We ARE T

Co

A Thirty Year Milton Keynes Bovine Celebration

By

David Ashford

Author's note:

In the early 1990's for a short time I had a weekly feature page called LIFESTYLE in our local newspaper The Milton Keynes Citizen. I also managed to persuade some national media to take the odd bit of my writing about the adolescent New City of Milton Keynes.

I wrote my Lifestyle Page using the pen-name of Jonathan Flie, Jonathan from my middle name of JOHN and Flie as in flie-on-the-wall, many of my newspaper articles were FLY-on-the-wall. (My real name is David by the way and I am here using it as I invite you to celebrate our city's bovine heritage.)

The original work has been out of print for many years. I am here, on the thirtieth birthday of my book, offering an updated version of the original text. So come and join me on a kaleidoscope through the adolescent New City of Milton Keynes while looking back from a somewhat middle-age City of Milton Keynes.

Enjoy:

David aka Jonathan Flie

This is not an introduction:
(From the original text)

The problem with any preface or introduction is that the average reader will simply skip it by in order to get into the meaty bits of the story.

But I do want you to read what I have to say here before you look at the main part of my text.

So this, therefore, is NOT an introduction ! OK ? Understand ? Of course it is really but just pretend for a moment will you, bear with me and stick with it.

I want to say, right at the outset of my this little book, that I am a strong supporter of Milton Keynes. My wife was actually born in the area but I proudly boast being one of the first immigrants to the New City, coming to live here in 1970. All of my children have been brought up in the city and I consider it to be a fine place to live. Fortunately, however, it is not Utopia – thank goodness for that ! But never let it be said in my hearing that the best thing to come out of Milton Keynes is the M1 !

I doubt there is such a thing as a Milton Keynes Fan Club but if there were then you could certainly put me down for an annual subscription.

I do not claim to be writing a historical study of the area. The late Sir Frank Markham's book, The History of Milton Keynes and District, published in two volumes and sold in every half decent bookshop, is the definitive work and if I had my way would be compulsory reading for every resident.

Instead this is supposed to be a fun look at the good, the bad and the ugly parts of this city of ours. A warts and all, to quote Oliver Cromwell, portrait because I think it is important we not only take pride in our achievements, of which there are many, but also learn to smile, indeed laugh, even cry at our follies.

I have centred the composition about the feature writing I have done over the past year or so in our local press. If parts of this book make you stop and think, if some of it makes you a little angry, then may be the odd paragraph will bring a smile to your face and something else will cause you to say, *I never knew that*, then I will have been successful.

There have been, over the past quarter of a century, many millions of words written about the New City of Milton Keynes and it would take a library of encyclopaedia to contain it all. But I hope that this view is just a little unique, putting things into a different perspective so to speak, but one thing for certain.

IT IS NOT THE CONCRETE COWS !

Right, it's time for me to stop babbling and get on with the story. So join me now as we kaleidoscope our way through the City of Milton Keynes.

I hope you enjoy the ride.

Jonathan Flie wishes to explain that he is a freelance writer and not in the employ of any newspaper or publisher. Although he produces the weekly Lifestyle Page for The Citizen, and has drawn upon much of his writing there for this book, the views expressed are entirely his own and are not necessarily the same as the newspaper's editor or proprietors.

A little thirty year update – We ARE The Concrete Cows:
On the original book's back cover the Milton Keynes Citizen sponsored its publication purchasing this advert.

The front cover of NOT THE CONCRETE COWS, the book's publisher was very clever using a photograph in negative of a concrete cow.

In the early days of Milton Keynes BBC presenter and DJ Noel Edmunds was always making jokes about how Milton Keynes had concreted over the fields on which cows had previously grazed meaning the real bovines had to be replaced with *concrete* cows !

Today We ARE The Concrete Cows.

The 1994 edition had a contents page but I have removed it, the cows ate it for breakfast, as I want you to dip in here and there as your fancy takes you, kaleidoscope through the pages and say MOO to our Concrete Cows.

THE FOLLIES OF MILTON KEYNES

In the Autumn of 1993 the Milton Keynes Citizen published a series of articles I put together on the follies of Milton Keynes. It was designed to be a tongue in the cheek smile at where we had got things wrong. I intentionally say WE and not THEY for if we can take a corporate pride and the things that are right in our city then we must be prepared to put our hands up and say *fair cop guv* when things are wrong.

The series attracted a good deal of readers' interest and the editor received a full mailbag. Some letters were in praise but others disagreed with my viewpoint. A few made suggestions for further articles, two which I took up to expand the series from six to eight episodes. Here we go then with a look at where WE have got it wrong. When you have read through my account get out your car and go and see them for yourself.

FOCUS ON THE FOLLIES STARTING WITH THE WINDMILL THAT NEVER TURNS

We are all, no doubt, familiar with the follies of English architecture, those enigmatic towers and castellated edifices erected in the grounds of many a stately home, the former Duke of Buckingham's estate at Stowe is positively littered with them.

The Oxford English Dictionary describes a folly as a costly structure which is totally useless. Perhaps that is a little unkind for many a folly was built in harmless fun and thousands every week derive innocent amusement by visiting those now preserved by the National Trust.

But what of the follies in Milton Keynes, nothing pre-twentieth century in this purpose built city of the modern age ?

No, I do not mean the concrete cows !

What I had more in mind with some of the landmarks we have come to love and hate, often in the same breath, was for their eccentricities and impracticability of design and purpose.

Some are amusing, others are downright frustrating. Some, in their time, aroused much public controversy while others climbed onto the back of our landscape almost unnoticed.

I have chosen the follies that come instantly to my mind but let me make it clear it is not my intention to be cruel or unkind, simply to bring each to attention in what I regard to be the true spirit of a folly.

My first choice of folly is the windmill that never turned. Well it's not a windmill exactly but a wind powered generator. Located at the junction of Watling Street and Faraday Drive this folly is a feature of Energy Park, an estate of purpose designed and built energy efficient homes.

But the trouble is this folly is one of the most inefficient articles in the entire city.

To return to the dictionary definition, goodness only knows what it cost to put up and certainly it is quite useless.

In Denmark I have seen entire hillsides covered with these generators, like farms of cultivated giant objects from a science fiction nightmare, all gently turning in the breeze.

But their junior emulator in Milton Keynes has failed to learn one important lesson from its mentors. In order to generate electricity the blades of the windmill have to turn around ! Those at Energy Park remain steadfastly static and have done so for many years.

Perhaps the mechanism is rusted up, surely the inactivity cannot be blamed upon a lack of wind. No, for unless my memory is seriously failing me, I remember the blades once revolving. Presumably the dwellings it was designed to serve now receive their electricity from less environmentally sound sources courtesy of National Power and Powergen.

It is rumoured the windmill was constructed ahead of its planning permission. Perhaps that is true, nobody seems to know for certain, it's one of those legends that tend to grow up about follies. At least no official in a pinstripe suit a so far demanded it be torn down.

But then why should it be? It is not doing anybody any harm is it ? It serves as a useful landmark on Watling Street and a true folly of Milton Keynes. Long may it remain.

A embarrassing thirty year update – We ARE the Concrete Cows:

The Windmill That Never Turns, my very first Lifestyle page in the Milton Keynes Citizen. It certainly captured readers' imaginations in 1994 but now in 2024 I am embarrassed. Yes, the readers loved it, The Windmill That Never Turns. The editor commissioned me to write about more follies within our adolescent New City. We were all short sighted.

But then why should it be ? It is not doing anybody any harm is it ? It serves as a useful landmark on Watling Street and a true folly of Milton Keynes. Long may it remain.

But it did not remain for long, it was taken down and has long since been completely forgotten. Energy Park became Shenley Lodge where I doubt the homes are any more energy efficient than elsewhere in Milton Keynes. On the estate is Caroline Haslett School. Do members of the school, do neighbours on Shenley Lodge know who Caroline Haslett was ?

Dame Caroline Harriet Haslett DBE, JP Born 17 August 1895 Died 4 January 1957, so aptly gave her name to the school. She was an electrical engineer and electricity industry administrator as well as being a champion of women's rights.

She is quoted as saying: *Way is being made by electricity for a higher order of women – women set free from drudgery, who have time for reflection; for self-respect. We are coming to an age when the spiritual and higher state of life will have freer development, and this is only possible when women are liberated from soul-destroying drudgery - I want every woman to have leisure to acquaint herself more profoundly with the topics of the day.'*

You know, I would quite like to see the windmill restored to its former location. I would very much like Shenley Lodge to revert to Energy Park then to lead all homes in Milton Keynes towards a higher level of energy efficiency.

Energy Park in the 1980's was all about being energy efficient and not saving our planet from global warming. It was not until May 1985 that a hole in the ozone layer was discovered. Milton Keynes was built as a city of trees for beauty and not to neutralise emissions. Milton Keynes likes to think it is a green city but it is not ! Greenish perhaps but not the deep colour we need within our kaleidoscope.

Where are the solar windmills in Milton Keynes today which do turn ? Where are the solar farms ? Not easy to find, are there any ? Where are the climate cowboys in Milton Keynes ? You won't have to look very far to find them !

THE FOLLY OF PORTWAY BRIDGE

If you concrete over vast tracts of farmland, as was done for the construction of Milton Keynes, you will upset the natural drainage and water table of the surrounding area. So what do you do then if you want to build a New City ?

Answer - build balancing lakes about the city to control the flow of rainwater and prevent flooding.

Lakes like Tongwell, Caldicotte and Willen are all man made safety valves for just this purpose.

Excavated between 1972 and 1974, from farmland on either side of the old course of the River Ouzel, Willen was the earliest balancing lake to be built. Over the next two decades it matured and naturalised into one of the beauty spots in Milton Keynes. The Peace Pagoda, bird sanctuary of North Lake, water sports centre of South Lake and of course, Willen Hospice have become some of the most celebrated and cherished landmarks in the area.

So from where pray came the sense in blundering a dual carriage way right through the middle of it all ?

It is true that H5 Portway was always in the strategic plan and no doubt looked quite harmless on two dimensional paper but its reality has ruined Willen and must be marked up as one of the greatest follies in Milton Keynes.

As I walked around Willen Lake early one summer morning with my wife I have to confess that for most of the time the road is obscured by trees and bushes, just occasionally emerging as an eyesore on the landscape. But trees and bushes cannot obscure the sound of dull rumbling traffic that is audible from most parts of the lake. The noise, I am afraid, took away all the enjoyment from the stroll in what were otherwise delightful surroundings.

When it first became apparent that a line on the planners map meant a busy main road being carved right through the middle of the area there was public protests but it was uncoordinated and stood no chance at all against the might of the Milton Keynes Development Corporation. So the road was built and the damage was done.

For my money this is one folly of Milton Keynes which should be torn down tomorrow and I am sure the powers that be would find no shortage of residents offering to do the demolition work for them !

A mixed thirty year update– We ARE The Concrete Cows:

Again readers loved that feature. KWFT – Doesn't exactly roll off the tongue. Keep Willen Forever Tranquil, that was the name of the campaign.

Driving over Portway Bridge today I have to confess I do not really notice Willen Lake beneath me. I don't think Milton Keynes City Council would find many signatures on any petition if KWFT were to seek this now well established bridge's demolition. Without it access across our city would be significantly hampered.

Is Willen tranquil all these years after my writing about its bridge ? I don't honestly have a clue. I used to go there and walk around the lake so often but not anymore. A foundation stone within Milton Keynes Development Corporation's Strategic Plan was there should be no parking charges within the New City. Today you have to PAY TO PARK if you want to visit

Willen Lake. Pardon me folks but you aint having any of my money ! Never mind Portway Bridge being a folly of Milton Keynes, Willen Lake has itself become one giant puddle of a folly !

PART AND PARCEL

Now whoever gave planning permission for that ? My reaction and I suspect one not so very dissimilar to others, when I first saw the Parcelforce sorting offices at Redmoor.

Before the trees matured and the more sober Burton Group's distribution centre obscured the view, Parcelforce stood out as a red blot on the landscape. I can fully understand why it was painted in such a vivid red, the corporate colour of the organisation, but oh dear it does look out of place.

Had it been the sister organisation of letter post putting up such a construction perhaps folk would have had a little more to say on the subject. But Postman Pat as well as delivering birthday cards and the occasional passionate letter, is the agent by which those dreaded bills for gas, electricity, telephone, council tax, credit cards and one thousand other demands plop through our letter boxes. But nobody sends bills by parcel post, only nice things wrapped in brown paper packages pass through the sorting house at Redmoor.

By the way I wonder if it is a coincidence that the area is known as Redmoor. Surely nobody had sufficient humour to call it red after Parcelforce's striking colour.

As Parcelforce's mission in life is a kindly one then perhaps we can forgive them this folly. But what if on privatisation they decide to change their corporate colour ? After all British Telecom went from bottle green to buttercup yellow and lately to a kind of faded battleship grey. Would they then need planning permission to repaint ?

THE BIG ONE

When the first foundations for Milton Keynes were set down more than a quarter of a century ago DIY superstores were in their infancy. Over the years their nationwide popularity has mushroomed and where better to ensure trading success than in a New City ?

Milton Keynes is blessed with all the major chains B & Q, Do It All, Great Mills and Homebase but the king by sheer measure of floor space has to be Texas on Rooksley. Rival companies may quibble as to who offers the lowest prices and bargains but Texas can surely rest secure in its boast to the biggest. But Oh dear, Tom, whoever designed your car park ?

The older residents of Milton Keynes will remember the original Texas store in Buckland Drive, Netherfield. When Tom felt the need for a bigger home the move to Rooksley was planned. Once there he still needed more space and so a new extension nearly doubled the size of the store.

Now all this is fine enough. The problem is the entrance to the store is at one extremity of the building while the exit and checkout tills are at the other. A turnstile prevents exit by the entrance and the other end of the store is protected by electronic doors that can only be activated from inside. The end result is that no matter where you park your car you are forced to walk the length of the store twice, once on the outside and once on the inside.

Of course in this country we enjoy a rather pulvinus climate and it is an established fact that most households DIY is done in times of bad weather when the great British public cannot go outside without running a danger of getting webbed feet. This is clearly understood by Texas Tom who has erected, for the shelter of his customers, a covered walkway the length of his shop front. Pity there is a great gap in the middle where the elements can deluge on all-comers as they hike from exit to entrance and vice versa.

Perhaps Tom may like to consider installing a moving pavement like they have in airports or perhaps station staff with cups of water to refresh the weary as is done in the London Marathon. I paced the length of the Texas store from entrance to exit and found it to be one hundred and seventy-five strides long. For the sake of mathematics let us of say that my pace is a yard long. That is a round trip of nearly one fifth of a mile just to buy a packet of screws ! As I look about my home I can now cost each DIY project not only in terms of hard earned cash needed to pay for it, nor in blood sweat and hammered fingernails employed in the construction, but the number of miles trekked about the Texas superstore in order to collect the materials.

Come on Tom, get your act together. Either organise checkout tills at both ends of your store or take a hammer from your own tool counter and knock a hole in the middle to make a new and more sensible entrance.

Until you do may I award you the honour of being one of the follies of Milton Keynes.

A thirty year update – We ARE The Concrete Cows: When I wrote that DIY aka Do-It-Yourself was a bit of a fun hobby for me. These days I am more into paying someone to do whatever that needs to be done about our home. If I actually do something myself it is to Winterhill I head and Wickes. Wickes where customer service and product quality jump out from every shelf and hit you. Texas Tom has long since vanished but his need for an Ordinance Survey Map is the modern day policy of B & Q, not to mention Homebase.

SO WHO WILL TAKE IT OFF OUR HANDS

At one time it sold cattle in pens down the side of Aylesbury Street. Then it moved to the site of the present-day Sainsbury's Supermarket in Oliver Road. Its next move was to Albert Street, behind the Co-op, before being relocated to its present location in Queensway . What is it ? It is Bletchley Market.

It is not entirely fair to say that Bletchley suffered under Milton Keynes Development Corporation but certainly it did not share in the spoils awarded to other parts of the city. The Queensway shopping area has to be a prime example. At one end, a folly in its own right, is Stanier Square, complete with tatty public notice boards, sparsely planted trees and decaying dais once intended to house a replica of a Brunel steam engine before somebody realised the costs involved. At the other end of the street, folly of follies, is Bletchley Market.

I suppose when this monstrosity was put up some architect thought it was very clever and no doubt was paid a handsome fee. But what a mess ! Looking like a giant mushroom field, it sprawls over the width of Queensway casting shadows across the adjacent shops.

A few years ago, in a fit of privatisation, the council sold off the franchise to the market firstly to Wendy Fair and then to Bray Associates the current lease holder.

Wendy Fair wanted to pull the whole edifice and reconstruct the area in the style of Victorian street market. Was this, I ask myself, why they lost the contract ? Is there some officials somewhere determined to cling, at all costs, onto this hideous mistake and architectural absurdity ? Isn't Bletchley long overdue for a facelift to its shopping area ? Couldn't something be done to brighten up Queensway and make it a more pleasing place to visit ? Is there somebody, somewhere who could take this folly off our hands ?

Who was it that purchased London Bridge and stuck it in the middle of the Arizona Desert? Do you think he would like Bletchley Market to put alongside it?

Well, we could always ask !

An embarrassed BIG TIME thirty year update – We ARE The Concrete Cows:

Today Bletchley Market as featured here as a folly has become a city legend. It may have been a joke, almost as big a joke as were our concrete cows, in 1994 but just look at the market joke Bletchley has today. Does anyone ever shop there ?

FOOD FOR THOUGHT

Is it not strange, even incongruous, that adjacent to one of the busiest shopping centres in England there should be another which is fast turning out to be the retail flop of the century ?

Just why is it when the Central Milton Keynes Shopping Centre attracts each Saturday a crowd double the size of even a very good gate from the football premier division the Milton Keynes Food Centre, on the other side of Midsummer Boulevard, attracts less than the number attending a game on a wet Saturday afternoon between two clubs languishing at the bottom of the Vauxhall Conference League ?

From the outside the Milton Keynes Food Centre is surely more pleasing to look at than its big brother and neighbour. Yet while the Central Milton Keynes Shopping Management Company can demand ever increasing rents and still fill every unit that becomes available there are shops in the food centre which have never had a customer and have never earned a single penny. For the noble few who soldier on business cannot be easy. Some of them are trading so badly they are being offered extended rent-free periods just to stay on.

So why will the people of Milton Keynes not give the Food Centre a chance ? When Tesco opened its store Kingston it was a hit from the first day. Could it be the design that is at fault ?

Built about a multi storey car park the shops form an outer facade but limit access so forcing customers to walkabout the perimeter. Could it be that people simply do not browse about food shops ? Window shoppers are, after all, the lifeblood of any city centre.

Would the centre stand a better chance if other lines were on offer ? Surely some of the businesses over the road would be happy to move to cheaper accommodation and tempt customers to cross Midsummer Boulevard.

First of all Milton Keynes Development Corporation and more lately managing agents on behalf of the borough council, have been trying without success for more than half a decade to kick start trading in the centre.

Of the follies I have chosen to feature in this series some are funny, others are stupid, but this one is just sad.

Thirty year update – We ARE The Concrete Cows:
Now simply gone !

A LASTING TRIBUTE FOR JAMES

Although Great Britain seldom manages is to excel in many areas of international sport we do, at least, totally dominate Formula One Motor Racing.

For grand prix after grand prix, the Williams cars from Abington show their heels to all comers, Damon Hill looks set to follow in the footsteps of his world champion father, Graham. Due credit must be given to Nigel Mansell, even if he does behave like a spoilt little boy, for the 1992 world championship, Silverstone provides the season's best circuit and even the ill-fated Bletchley Footwork team deserved some points for their efforts !

So where in all this is the folly ?

When I first began to compose my series on the follies of Milton Keynes I deliberately left this out by way of respect to the late James Hunt who was so suddenly taken from us right at the time I was putting pen to paper. However, many readers wrote into the Milton Keynes Citizen asking that I turn my attention in his direction. So James, if you are looking down from the great Grand Prix circuit in the sky please forgive me as we smile at the James Hunt Racing Centre and award it the honour of being included as one of our follies.

When the circus came to town, with the red and white marquee styled centre building, The James Hunt Racing Centre promised to bring the nation's most successful, yet most expensive sport into the budget of the average person. But before this ambitious project had even completed the warmup lap it was forced into the pit lane, closing its doors in receivership. Sadly, no future Damon Hill or Nigel Mansell would ever graduate from its driving school .

James Hunt was an electric personality, first rate grand prix commentator and world class driver, clinching the 1976 championship from Niki Lauda in the nail-biting finish to the season. Is this folly then a fitting epitaph to his career ?

Had things gone to plan the centre's prominent position adjacent to the main A5 trunk road with its vivid red and white big top, looking to all as if the circus are come to town, would have been a proud landmark for Milton Keynes instead of now being a source of fun.

I drove down to the centre at Rooksley while writing this feature where I found the car park totally overgrown with weeds and a roughly painted sign on the gate declaring the circuit to be CLOSED. As I took out my camera and notebook a burly security guard emerged to see me on my way.

So what should become of this folly ? Indeed should anything be done at all or would it be better left to continue the rot that has already started to set in ?

When the US prison authorities closed the maximum security gaol Alcatraz, in San Francisco Bay, they feared the already notorious island becoming the folly of the West Coast. A competition was run to decide what should be done with the site. Some pretty wacky ideas were submitted but eventually it was decided to turn it into a museum.

Now, instead of jeering at it, thousands flock every week to view the artefact of a bygone era when some of America's most notorious gangsters were incarcerated in the bleak regime on the Alcatraz Rock.

So what about a museum on the site of the ill-fated James Hunt Racing Centre ? A museum to celebrate and preserve the glorious history of British motor racing. It would after all make an ideal location and there would surely be no shortage of exhibits to put on display.

Thousands would want to visit such an attraction, turning a bankrupt, pathetic folly into a thriving tourist venue which would be a credit to Milton Keynes .

James Hunt is on record saying how much he regretted his involvement with the centre. It is such a pity that he took these sentiments to his grave but what a great tribute it would be, not only to his career but also to the entire sport, to resurrect the folly as the James Hunt Museum of Motor Racing.

Postscript: (From 1994 – not 2024)
Since I wrote my feature the James Hunt Racing Centre plans have been revealed to revamp it in alternative vein but I still think it would have made an excellent site for a racing museum.

THIS REALLY GIVES ME THE HUMP

I cannot help but wonder if it is ever intended to finish off the traffic management scheme introduced into West Bletchley more than five years ago.

Bletchley never did do all that well out of Milton Keynes Development Corporation did it ?

Within the southern tip of the city, what money did filter through managed to pass by the West Bletchley area. That was until some planner, somewhere, conceived

the West Bletchley traffic management scheme and spared no expense on this stupidity.
The plan involved the construction of a series of steep ramps and road narrows, closing the junction of Tattenhoe Lane with Buckingham Road, placing a weight limit on Shenley Road and revising the Whaddon Way/Watling Street intersection. Talk to residents and most will tell you that the scheme is a total failure but then nobody in any position of authority has ever bothered to talk with them.

Shenley Road still carries an unfair measure of traffic with the weight limit far from always being observed. The ramps are exceedingly fierce damaging car tracking and exhaust mountings, while those combined with road narrows cause unnecessary traffic congestion. But the greatest frustration of all is the simple fact that since its introduction the scheme would look to have been completely forgotten. Forgotten, that is, before it was even finished ! The measures put down to prevent traffic turning right out of Whaddon Way onto Watling Street are nothing more than a series of rough blocks of wood now filthy with age, and some hastily erected warning signs. Temporary for more than five years. But then I suppose time itself is relative for signs on Shenley Road announcing new ramps have been in existence for just as long. How much time is needed before they become old ramps ?

White triangles ineffectively glued to the roads soon lifted on car tyres only to be transplanted along the length of the road. Most have long since disappeared altogether. Now parts of the ramps themselves are starting to disintegrate, coping stones never correctly cemented into the ground are starting to move while the substructure is collapsing under the weight of the traffic.

It is difficult to imagine a similar situation being allowed to develop in say Stony Stratford or Central Milton Keynes so why West Bletchley ? Has the highways department lost all interest in its scheme, are the planners ashamed to put their hands up and claim responsibility for this folly ? What about local elected councillors who should be keeping a watching brief on their ward ? Or is it just another absurdity the long-suffering residents of Bletchley will have to put up with while other parts of the city savour the cherry from Milton Keynes cake ?

THE FORGOTTEN LANDMARKS OF MILTON KEYNES

When we think of landmarks within this fine New City of ours we tend to call to mind things that have appeared on the landscape only within recent years. The Point, Central Milton Keynes Railway Station or perhaps the Church of Christ the Cornerstone with its dome and cross standing proudly high and visible for miles around. But we must realise the planners and developers did not construct Milton Keynes entirely upon virgin land, somethings were there before.

I followed up my series in the Milton Keynes Citizen writing on the follies of Milton Keynes by drawing readers attention to some of the older and perhaps forgotten landmarks beginning with Leon Bridge.

LEON BRIDGE:

Everyday thousands upon thousands of rail passengers thunder over it and hundreds of cars vans and lorries passed beneath it, even the odd pedestrian still walks along its footpath yet few realised its significance. Officially it is the Denby Hall Railway Bridge but to those who know its story it will always be Leon Bridge.

In 1882, at the age of thirty-two Herbert Samuel Leon brought his new wife Fanny to Bletchley and went about setting himself up as the local squire. He purchased Bletchley Park together with the adjoining properties of Home Farm and Denby Hall Farm. His land extended over much of present day Bletchley, from Shenley Road to Watling Street and from Church Green Road to the railway.

He was determined to make and leave his mark upon the area both of which he succeeded in. At the extreme South of Milton Keynes one of our schools still bears his name, an area of ground in Fenny Stratford given to the local children to play upon and is still known as Leon Rec. And then there are Leon Cottages and Leon Avenue. But he did not confine his activities to what is now South Milton Keynes he was a director of the Wolverton Tram Company, justice of the peace and liberal member of parliament for North Buckinghamshire from 1891 to 1895. Wherever Leon could make his mark locally he seized the opportunity as he laid down the foundations for a dynasty to rule Bletchley as a personal kingdom. (In fact the dynasty lasted only for his generation as his son George sold the family's Milton Keynes properties in 1933 but that is another story.) One place where he literally carved his name was on the Denby Hall Railway Bridge.

Approach the bridge from the south and upon the right hand upright, obscured by the undergrowth. British Rail get your shears out, you will read engraved:

Prior to September 1838 the southern part of this railway terminated at this bridge when passengers were conveyed by coach to Rugby where they re-joined the railway to Birmingham. This commemoration by Sir Herbert Leon Bart of Bletchley Park by kind permission of the LR MW railway August 1920.

Kind permission is a little interesting for Leon and the railway were not exactly the best of friends. Some years earlier he had taken the company to court in a civil action for depositing soot from their steam engines on his land. The court found in his favour but awarded damages of just one shilling - 5 pence.

But thanks to Leon the important part of railway history and the role of Milton Keynes within its infancy are preserved.

A railway journey from London to Birmingham in 1838 was more than a little different from today. No Intercity 125's in those days, gliding along at speeds of up to 125 miles an hour. The lines from London Euston to Denby Hall and from Rugby to Birmingham were opened 9th April 1838. Two obstacles prevented a continuous railway journey. The first was a viaduct to cross the River Ouzel at Wolverton and the second the construction of the tunnel Kilsby. Both were monumental projects even by the side of the rest of the line and forced a five month delay to completion during which time horse-drawn coaches connected passengers on the four hour journey between the two stations.

Denby Hall was chosen as the terminus because it was there that the railway crossed the Watling Street but no prospect proper facilities were installed for the passengers. There was no sanitation, no proper accommodation, tents often being the only overnight shelter and mud was everywhere. Railway construction workers were billeted at Denby Hall and drunken brawls were commonplace. One passenger described Bletchley as a small miserable village where those disappointed at getting from Denby Hall must not expect to find accommodation, even for their dog !

The only place to take any refreshment was at the Denby Hall Inn which had the most terrible reputation for previously harbouring highwaymen and criminals and for generally being a bawdy house. At least three murders took place in the locality which two centuries earlier had been the site for the local gallows.

All these unpleasantries must have spurred the railway company to complete the line as quickly as possible.

But all this took place twenty years before Herbert Leon was born and fifty years before he brought his family to Bletchley. Had he been around at the time perhaps the passengers would have enjoyed a slightly better time, not only from Leon's philanthropic nature but also by way of his careful eye to the profit that could be made out of entertaining the travellers.

A thirty year update – We ARE The Concrete Cows:
Within my writing about Milton Keynes I speak a lot about Sir Frank Markham and his twin volume work The History Of Milton Keynes And District. I was a student at Milton Keynes Teacher Training College when he published these works and am proud to have attended two lectures he gave on his writing. Sir Frank had served as Member of Parliament for North Buckinghamshire and it was within Her Majesty Queen Elizabeth II's Coronation Honours that he was awarded his knighthood.

I was the student member on the college board of governors. Lady Markham was also a board member. We would sit together at meetings.

When I was writing Not The Concrete Cows, particularly referring to Leon Bridge, she gave me permission to use her husband's work in support of my own.

The words placed on the bridge are now totally obscured by trees and shrubbery which you can see to my left. Also with the level of traffic it would be dangerous to try to read them.

So many, many times I have tried to get authorities to engage with this iconic part of our city's heritage and to reproduce them somewhere else nearby.

Prior to September 1838 the southern part of this railway terminated at this bridge when passengers were conveyed by coach to Rugby where they re-joined the railway to Birmingham. This commemoration by Sir Herbert Leon Bart of Bletchley Park by kind permission of the LR MW railway August 1920.

Sadly, I have failed to get anyone to engage !

BABY BOOM AND THE DEATH OF LEGEND:

I moved to Milton Keynes way back in 1970 when, other than in the minds of the planners, the area then consisted of little more than Stony Stratford and Wolverton in the north, Bletchley in the south and the splattering of villages in the middle. There was no Milton Keynes Borough Council at the time while places like Newport Pagnell and Woburn Sands remained firmly outside the umbrella of what was glibly called the designated area.

When I asked the clerk at Birmingham New Street Station for a ticket to Milton Keynes he scratched his head, consulted a directory then thrusted a slip of card at me which said: *The nearest you can get to is Bletchley, take a bus from there.*

But Bletchley is Milton Keynes isn't it I protested.

"Dunnow mate - next please."

I had understood that Milton Keynes derived its name from a poet and an economist, quite a common misunderstanding in the early days, but once on Bletchley station I was to learn different. There I parted with seven shillings and six pence, yes it was pre decimal in those days, at the book kiosk to purchase of copy up the local Ordnance Survey Map.

From this document I learned that Milton Keynes was very much in existence, there it was on the map possibly in existence since the Doomsday Book, and not just something in the minds of the moguls at the Development Corporation, even if British Rail had never heard of it. So, once I had a chance to settle into my new home I set off in search Milton Keynes.

Take a bus, the man at New Street Station had said. He must have been joking ! In 1970 there were just two buses a week from Bletchley to Milton Keynes. In those pre-city days you either used the car, walked or simply stayed at home.

When I eventually found my way to Milton Keynes I discovered it to be a quaint little village sort of in the middle of the acres of land mass which would eventually take on its name. And dominating the village was the Swan public house. Well it was lunchtime after all so a quick visit didn't seem all that much out of order. “It's a bit quite in here today landlord”, there was only myself and two old farmers with their pints of Guinness.

He smiled: “Three of you, that's a crowd in this pub ! The problem is this village is dying on its feet and my trade along with it.”

He went on to explain that over the past decade the village population had been steadily falling and was now down to only just above one hundred souls. But the fortune was perfectly secure so long as the tree remained.

Tree ? I puzzled.

Taking me by the arm to the doorway, he pointed out the large tree towering over the green in front of the pub. “That's a pretty important tree. Legend says if it is ever cut down there will be no more babies born in Milton Keynes.”

I am no botanist but I had to agree with him it certainly looked a splendid specimen, probably centuries old. Certainly nobody alive would have been old enough to remember it being planted.

I could not help wondering how the legend had come about, my host did not seem to know its origin or if it was true or not. Just supposing it was then maybe the planners were taking on something of a major problem by naming the city after this particular village.

Presumably the intention was for the splendid New City of Milton Keynes to last for at least the next thousand years, do trees live that long ? I doubt it. OK, so I was an immigrant and the plan was to attract nearly a quarter of a million others like me but they would have to come a time when the city would need to become self-sufficient as far as population was concerned. What would happen when the tree reached the end of its life ? Would the fastest developing area in Europe suddenly becomes sterile ? It was not a prospect to dwell on.

Sadly, the days of this special tree were numbered. After seeing the area as a parliamentarian stronghold in the civil war, after watching the monarchy supporting generations past, having shed its leaves every autumn before bursting forth the next spring in a profusion of green it was soon to be no more. After centuries of being at the very heart of Milton Keynes it was found to be so dangerous that it was decided it just had to be cut down. I am glad that I was not the appointed axeman or the tree surgeon who signed its death warrant. What an awesome responsibility ?

But the Rector of Milton Keynes, now the Reverend David Lung, continues to christen babies in the Parish Church of All Saints as have done his predecessors since the ceremony was first introduced into the church. In 1563 records show that the village had just thirty-one households, new housing developments have multiplied this many times with all using the services of maternity unit at Milton Keynes General Hospital. One has but to look at the birth announcements in the local press to see that the city is providing for itself a fine and healthy younger generation.

So the legend was all fiction then ? It would appear at first sight so to be. But when I took a visit to Milton Keynes for the first time in several years in order to pen this particular little feature and there in the front of the Swan is a brand new tree proudly taking the place of its great-great-great-great grandfather. It was quite reassuring to find it there and to understand that the legend looks to have been transferred to it. This fine young specimen has for certain a long life ahead of it and will see the city through a fair few generations to come.

FORGOTTEN BUT NOT GONE:

As I put pen to paper each week to write my page in the Milton Keynes Citizen I could not help but cast my mind back to when I first came to live in Milton Keynes. (I know I keep on about being the first generation of immigrants to this city but I am proud of that fact.) Of course there are many who having been born in the area have lived here much longer than I.

Shortly after I moved in I was given a special tour of the city's early foundations by one of the then town councillors, Bletchley And Urban District Town Council. I have to confess to drawing upon my memories of that tour in order to help put together much of my writing on the forgotten landmarks of Milton Keynes.

I wonder how many of my readers can share their own memories of some of the landmarks from my tour: Scott of Bletchley - makers of the world's finest cooked meats, Queen’s Pool, Cowley and Wilson Garage on Buckingham Road, Spurgeon Church, and The Three

Bridges all sadly or no longer with us. But one remains today against which my host shared a fine little anecdote is Fenny Lock on the Grand Union Canal I have pleasure in now passing this on to you.

Stony Stratford in the north of the city established itself about the turnpike road map of the early industrial revolution but even with the new road improvements it was still very costly to move freight by stage waggon. Enter the age of the canal. By 1830 Britain had over four thousand miles of canals and barges capable of carrying loads of up to one hundred tonnes.

The story of the canal in Milton Keynes began one June evening in 1792 in a room above an inn Stony Stratford. There met the Marquis of Buckingham, several local men of substance and one James Barnes, at engineer who had worked with the father of England's canals, James Brindley. Barnes proposed linking London with the industrial Midlands by way of Linslade, Soulbury, Stoke Hammond, Fenny Stratford, Simpson, Woughton, The Woolstones, Linford and Wolverton. He had costed the project at £500,000 pounds. The meeting agreed to his plan and promised the finance. In April 1975 parliament passed the Grand Junction Canal Act (The canal was renamed Grand Union in 1929) and work began immediately at both ends of the intended waterway .

Only two years later, Saturday the 31st May 1800, the Marquis of Buckingham officially opened the first section of the canal from Tring to Fenny Stratford. It was a carnival of a day with bands, cannons firing, and ringing of church bells together with a grand parade of members of the Buckinghamshire Militia.

Charges were set by freight on the canal at three quarters of a penny per ton per mile for coal, half a penny per ton per mile for livestock, a quarter of a penny per ton per mile for limestone, one penny per mile for all other goods .

The Marquis of Buckingham and his fellow shareholders looked forward to enjoying considerable profits from their investments. And they were not disappointed, in 1832 a £1 share in the company had risen in value to £2.42 and a dividend of 13% was declared.

So Fenny Stratford saw the opening of the Grand Junction Canal and with it came a period of some considerable change in the area. But it is not just the initial opening that entitles Fenny to claim fame within the history of Britain's inland waterways. The lock opposite the Red Lion is a smallest lock in the entire system, adjusting the water by only four inches .

My host on that original tour explained there had been an error of engineering planning. The two sections of the canal navigated to meet up left red faces when it was found that the two levels were a different heights. Fenny Lock was installed to correct the error. This explanation is widely accepted and has formed a legend among those who live in its locality. It's a nice little story and I rather hope that it is true but the odds are against it.

The more accepted explanation among those who profess to be authorities on this particular part of our heritage claimed that the lock was installed to correct an engineering difficulty but not one of the dug levels. (There is debate as to if it is a four inch lock or twelve inches. it doesn't really matter.) It was intended to run the course of the canal all the way north to Cosgrove without a lock but that would have entailed banking up the canal side by several feet all the way from Fenny Stratford to Woughton. No matter how the engineers tried to overcome the problem the bank persisted in leaking. They were faced with either cementing the bank in order to make it watertight or installing a lock so reducing the water level. They chose the latter.

My father-in-law recalls as a boy being taught in school that the engineer responsible for the Fenny Stratford section of the waterways committed suicide. It would appear that whatever the error he could not face up to the disgrace. So Fenny Lock has gone down in history both as the site of the official opening of the waterway and as a cover up for a monumental engineering mistake.

HOWE PARK AND SAINT GILES TATTENHOE:
For as long as I have lived in the area, nearly quarter of a century now, I have known somewhere at the back of my mind of its existence but it was only recently, and then quite by chance, that I came upon the Church of Saint Giles, Tattenhoe. Together with the adjacent Howe Park Wood it forms one of the oldest and most forgotten landmarks within the City of Milton Keynes. It is only with the recent extension of the grid road system

into the south-west flank of Milton Keynes that the church and surrounding land have become at all accessible. Even today there is still no road to the church, the closest regular access is to the tiny and ancient hamlet of Tattenhoe from where it lies is through two fields along a farm track.

The existing church dates from 1540 but is built upon the site of a much earlier sanctuary. Little has changed over the centuries, no mains electricity reaches this particular part of the most modern city in Europe so church services still rely upon candlelight. How many places, even in the remotest of areas, remain so totally untouched by twentieth century technology ? Indeed evensong is only heard every other Sunday between Rogation (mid May) and harvest time. Congregations are tiny, of course, and not able to support a vicar of their own so services come under the charge of Reverend Giles Godber, minister of the adjacent church at Loughton. I am much indebted to the Reverend Godber for his help in putting together the account of this particular forgotten landmark.

But it wasn't always like this. From Roman times the wood at Howe Park was a vital resource to the surrounding inhabitants. Tattenhoe expanded at the time of the Norman Conquest as the local population increased. The Doomsday Survey of 1086 listed Howe Park as woodland of one hundred acres in the Parish of Shenley. Venison was an important food during the mediaeval period and the wood a significant source of deer. Muntjac deer still live in the area today along with rabbits, foxes, badgers, wood mice, weasels and thousands of butterflies.

Compared to the wood, Saint Giles Church is but an infant. It is possible that Howe Park is an example of a primary woodland, a surviving fragment of woodland that developed over the whole of Britain after the last Ice Age, eleven thousand years ago ! Adjacent to the remains of the mediaeval ditch that once surrounded the entire wood is an oak tree which could be the oldest living thing in Milton Keynes. The Tattenhoe Oak.

Two fascinating legends are told about Tattenhoe. Firstly, that Thomas Becket spent time at the Tattenhoe Manor House and worshipped in the original church some years before he became Archbishop of Canterbury and was subsequently murdered in his own cathedral. The second legend claims that a secret passage once existed between the church and Shenley Park. Although neither entrance nor exit are now apparent, perhaps maybe parts still remain deep underground with their mysteries and ghosts from those far off generations.

Tattenhoe declined at a similar time to the consecration of Saint Giles. The reason for the downturn in the area's fortunes is unclear, perhaps it came as a result of the Dissolution or maybe because of the plague but when Milton Keynes Development Corporation purchased the wood and surrounding land in 1968 it was all but extinct. But while other areas of the city developed planners left this sector dormant. Only in recent months have things started to change.

The infrastructure of the roads is now in place, the redway footpaths are reaching out and the wood has been opened as part of the Milton Keynes Parks Trust. New housing is rising on the very ground upon once stood the original village and, such is progressive, Safeway's is developing a major new supermarket due to open next summer. (Safeways – now Morrissons)

So things are very soon going to change. Tattenhoe will again become a thriving community. Howe Park will be frequented by many whiling away their leisure hours and thereafter Saint Giles will ring out to the chorus of a hearty congregation. Plans are in hand for a new road from the grid system direct to the church, water and electricity will for the first time in history serve the sanctuary. The ancient moat, so overgrown and stagnant, will be restored. Land adjacent to Safeway Supermarket is reserved for new style church to accommodate a much larger congregation while Saint Giles will continue with its tradition.

When Milton Keynes was in its infancy Mabel Smith, wife of Reverend Hilton Smith, then Vicar of Whaddon and Tattenhoe, looked forward to this time when she wrote: *Someday perhaps this little church will serve a larger congregation. Of those who come from city great to join us with song.*

The future of Tattenhoe is bright and perhaps it is fitting the planners left the area until the near completion of Milton Keynes before wrapping the arms of the New City about it. Now the oldest living thing The Tattenhoe Oak joins hands with the newest of the New City to mark the conclusion of one of the greatest and most successful planning population migrations in history.

A happy thirty year update – We ARE The Concrete Cows:

The church was never built at Westcroft, Saint Giles Church now has electricity and all the rest, it is a thriving centre within a lovely part of our city. The parkland is a very popular dog walking area, it is the favourite playground for my own Doggie Barnaby.

JURASSIC CLASSIC:

Steven Spielberg Jurassic Park ? Forget it !

Crowds flocking to the cinema screens up and down the country, media hype, marketing bandwagons covering everything. Anyone would think that Mr Spielberg and Universal Studios invented the species. Well the silver screen mogul is very much mistaken, Milton Keynes has had its own Jurassic classics for years !

Every British Rail passenger travelling up and down the mainline through Bletchley could be forgiven for thinking themselves a victim of a time warp. Either that or perhaps they wonder if the eight thirty-two out of Euston has taken a wrong turning and ended up in Hollywood California. For there, snarling at all and towering thirty feet above its surroundings is a life size tyrannosaurus rex !

But this specimen is, for the most part, friendly and being constructed out of reinforced concrete not likely to terrorise anyone. Living at the bottom of Leon School's playing field this particular dinosaur was built by over one hundred youngsters under the direction of local artist Bill Billings. During the spring and summer of 1991 they dug out the foundations an erected a steel frame support before casting the beast in concrete.

Although Central Television showed an initial interest in the statute it has entered the landmark scene of Milton Keynes and been taken so much for granted but it is all but forgotten. T Rex is not the only one of Bill Billing's Jurassic creations to roam the city. Are few miles along Marlborough Street, at Peartree Bridge, is triceratops again sculptured in concrete and this particular dinosaur came to live in Milton Keynes fifteen years ago .

Standing in the grounds of the Interaction project at the Old Rectory, Peartree Bridge, this dinosaur has been featured in a Bon Jovi video and was, for a time, the subject of the most popular selling postcard of Milton Keynes. Unfortunately the trees along the V8 have matured now to the point where the sculpture can no longer be seen from the road. But next time you are in the area turn off towards Waterside and admire this particular landmark.

So Mr Spielberg you may become a legend in your own time but so, in Milton Keynes, has Bill Billings. Then when your Jurassic Park is consigned to the discount shelves of the video stores and repeated every Boxing Day on our television Bill's creations will still be in their youth. And who knows Bill may have another Jurassic classic in mind to graze the plains of our city !

A thirty year update of shame and disrespect ! – We ARE The Concrete Cows:

The original idea for Leon Dinosaur was that of Headmaster Bruce Abbott. He handed the idea to me saying my year group was to make it happen. I engaged community artist Bill Billings and work began.

After Headmaster Abbott retired he school's new dinosaur management moved this statue to what was then an adventure playground. It was no longer the first thing seen by train passengers travelling from London to our city.

A freedom of information request I made to Milton Keynes Council claimed that from this time on Leon Dinosaur became the property of Bletchley and Fenny Stratford Town Council. However, this body denied it was aware of its ownership.

Leon Dinosaur then fell into a terrible state of neglect and demise.

With both Headmaster Bruce Abbott and Community Artist Bill Billings having passed on I felt it was my duty to rescue our city's precious icon. I had huge public support but neither Milton Keynes Council nor Bletchley and Fenny Stratford Town Council showed any interest. Within the Lakes Estate Redevelopment Leon Dinosaur was destroyed. It has now gone down in the history of our city shrouded in shame and total disrespect !

QUEEN ELANOR PASSED THIS WAY:

When the Milton Keynes Development Corporation started planting roads and houses about the city considerable care was taken in their naming. This is greatly to their credit and replace the rather haphazard lottery by which previous assortments of local authorities christened things in their days. Somewhere in the depths of the borough council's archives exists a list explaining the source of each and every name.

As Watling Street swings away from the old Roman route to bypass the town centre of Stony Stratford it takes the name Queen Eleanor Street. The significance of this name dates back to 1291.

Eleanor was the beautiful Queen of Edward I who reigned from 1272 to 1307. They were married when she was just ten years old and Edward fifteen, the marriage being arranged for political reasons by their parents. Thirty-five years later, while following her husband on a journey to Scotland she fell ill in Nottinghamshire and died on the 29th November 1290.

The bereaved and devastated Edward had her body brought back to Westminster Abbey where she still rests today. At every place the funeral cortege stopped for the night King Edward ordered that a cross be erected. These were built in Lincoln, Grantham, Stamford, Geddington near Kettering, Northampton, Stony Stratford, Woburn, Dunstable, St Albans, Waltham, Cheap and perhaps the most famous, at Charing - Charing Cross.

Only three crosses still remain those at Northampton, Gedddington and Charring. The Milton Keynes cross at Stony Stratford disappeared during the civil war, probably in 1646.

Imagine the imposing royal procession as it passed through Stony Stratford. There was, of course, the King himself but also priests, courtiers and mourners all travelling in horse drawn waggons. There was the bier draped in purple and black. It is thought that the king and his entourage probably spent the night in one of the early high street inns.

The spot chosen for the cross was about a quarter of a mile south of the bridge over the river towards the town where a small bronze plaque today records:

Near to this spot stood the cross erected by King Edward I to mark the place in Stony Stratford where the body of Queen Eleanor rested on his way from Harby in Nottinghamshire to Westminster Abbey in 1290.

Having taken the trouble to research the story, erect a commemorative plaque and name the road after this Plantagenet Queen I wonder why the Development Corporation did not think to go one step further and reconstruct the cross after an absence of more than three centuries. After all it would not have been too difficult to model it upon the design of the three remaining and restore the landmark. There is insufficient space on the present-day pavement but as no one can be fully certain of the exact location why not use the green at the end of the town where Queen

Eleanor Street joins Watling Street ? Such would provide a fine landmark at the northern end of Stony Stratford and the City of Milton Keynes.

But the Milton Keynes Development Corporation is no more and neither the Borough Council nor the Commission for New Towns are likely to pick up the challenge. But there may be a local group, perhaps a business that has profited from the coming of Milton Keynes, who would be prepared to sponsor the remaking of the lost Queen and her cross. It is an interesting challenge and who knows.

DO YOU REMEMBER

Although I consider myself to be a feature writer and not a historian there can be no doubt that my historical research in Milton Keynes generated the greatest interest of all I published in the Milton Keynes Citizen. When my series on Wartime Milton Keynes was printed I received something like twenty letters every week.

I hasten to clarify the fact that I was not born until well after the end of World War Two at that my own memories of the area go back only until the early days of the New City.

Remembering those early days when I first made my way to Milton Keynes I thought I would like to write and tell those who more recently moved into the city what life was like living upon a giant building site. Of course I had my own memories but nothing written down and so I turned to the Commission for New Towns, who inherited all the Milton Keynes Development Corporation archives, for help. I may as well have tried to penetrate NATO defence headquarters ! It would appear that some bureaucrat, somewhere, decided all those records should be subject to national security and locked away for thirty years ! Brilliant and so what looked to me a promising series and one that most certainly would have generated a lot of local interest was confined to just four episodes.

However, I had tremendous fun writing them and hope you enjoy reading them. Here they are.

DIAL-A-BUS:

Poor old Milton Keynes City Bus does not always enjoy the best of press coverage does it ? But may I dare to suggest its critics take a look back to the infancy of this city. It could be members of today's travelling public do not know they are born !

The border of Milton Keynes is now larger than the area planned back in the 1960's for development of the city. Newport Pagnell, Olney and Woburn Sands have all been added into the designated area which originally included Wolverton, Stony Stratford Bletchley and all the villages in between. But no efficient public transport system used to link them up.

When the old Bletchley Urban District Council and the Greater London Council got together to put up the Lakes Estate only four buses a day connected it with Bletchley's Queensway. That was in spite of the fact that the new development was 20% the size and the entire town !

During a few weeks I lived in Woburn Sands Sundays meant being confined to barracks. I didn't drive at the time, the train shut down on the sabbath and buses had yet to find their way on the Bow Brickhill Road. But when I moved to Tinkers Bridge, an early estate then on extremity of the southern development, the corporation housing officer laughed when he learned I had no transport at my own. The first purchase I therefore made on my Barclaycard was a push bike !

There were just three buses a day in the in the early 1974 from Tinkers Bridge to Bletchley, one of which actually ventured as far as the new estate of Eaglestone. But this was a luxury compared to places like Wavendon, Great Linford and Broughton who had only as many buses in a week.

There were no such things as redways in the early 1970's, indeed there was little of the present grid road system in place, as I pedalled the weary and saddle-sore miles to and from Bletchley each day.

The very few buses that were run courtesy of United Counties, a division of National Buses operated to their own convenience, apparently ignorant any passenger needs.
Rescue came in the shape of the Milton Keynes Development Corporation sponsored project Dial-a-Bus.

Six Mercedes minibuses, not unlike the present-day street shuttles, were purchased and painted in vivid yellow. Two-way radio sets were installed in the drivers cabs and dial-a-bus emblazoned down each side. For those homes not on the telephone, the majority of the new estates in those pre BT days when it took an average of three months for a domestic connection, special call boxes were installed under lamp posts in every street giving a direct link to DAB, dial-a-bus, control.

The service was set up to run on Tinkers Bridge, Netherfield and Bean Hill. When you wanted to travel all that was needed was to telephone dial-a-bus where the controller would make radio contact with the nearest vehicle and dispatch it to your home. The bus would actually pull up right outside your front door and toot its horn.

Tickets were only about 20% higher than the normal buses and a tiny fraction of those charged by taxi operators. In just a short space of time dial-a-bus became very popular, quickly filling to capacity. Something had to be done as people were spending longer and longer cruising about the estates, picking up additional passengers, before actually heading off towards their destination. A slight revision was made and the bus no longer pulled up at your door, instead the controller would offer an estimated time of arrival then asked you to meet it at the end of the road.

The dial-a-bus was only ever intended to be a stopgap, to provide a limited form of public transport before more formal routes could be established, to give the planners some idea of the timings and destinations the local residents were likely to support.

The Milton Keynes Development Corporation never regarded their brainchild particularly highly and certainly it must have cost a small fortune to run. So inevitably the system was closed down, the telephones removed from lamp posts and the vehicles pensioned off to that great bus depot in the sky.

But just one thing still remains.

Have you ever wondered about the strange road layout at Bletchley Railway Station ? Next time you are down that way stand with your back against Bletchley Park and look towards the station across Sherwood Drive. What possible use could there be for the slip road on your left ? No traffic uses it, it doesn't go anywhere, and double yellow lines prevent it being used for parking. This was the Bletchley terminus for the dial-a-bus and remains as a reminder of one of the features in the early history in the New City of Milton Keynes.

Oh And By The Way - London Back For 25p:
In 1970 British Rail introduce an evening return fare to London of just 25p. To take advantage of the price passengers could not leave Bletchley before 5:00pm and had to return by midnight. Every night dozens travelled down to the capital by way of this special rate.

I travelled on the night flyer to see the Tutankhamun exhibition at the British Museum and no less than six times to watch the rock opera Jesus Christ Superstar.

The opera has, of course, now closed and the artefacts of King Tut returned to Cairo. Seemingly with them has gone British Rail's discounted evening tickets. The last time I took the train to London I needed a mortgage to pay for my ticket.

NO AIRPORT HERE:

Season travellers of the airways will be familiar with the coded baggage tags that ensure one's suitcases arrive via the same aircraft with their owners and at the same destination.

LHR - London Heathrow   SFO - San Francisco
LAX - Los Angeles
JFK - New York Kennedy   LGW - London Gatwick

But what about LMK - London Milton Keynes ? Daily flights to New York, Cairo, Rome, Bombay and one hundred other far away destinations ?

Don't smile because this was very nearly the case ! If the now infamous Robert Maxwell, one-time Labour Member of Parliament for our area had, had his way intercontinental jets would be constantly roaring overhead.

Thirty years ago advanced planning was calling for a new airport to relieve the strain that anticipated demand would place on Heathrow and Gatwick over the next century. One of the best options looked to be building London's third airport at Cublington just south of the area designated for the construction of a New City.

Within the triangle of roads between Stewkley, Wing and Cublington is the site of a former World War Two airfield from which the Royal Air Force flew against the might of the Third Reich. It is up on this site the proposed airport was planned, only six miles from Milton Keynes. But the project intended extending to a staggering seven and a half thousand acres, bulldozing flat everything in the way. The destruction would have included obliterating the entire village of Stewkley, claimed to be the longest village in England, and rehousing it's eleven hundred residents.

North Buckinghamshire is already on the North Atlantic route with dozens of heavy jets passing overhead everyday but these are all well on their way to their initial cruising altitude, flying sufficiently high to be relatively unnoticed. Had the airport come here instead of Stansted then living in Milton Keynes would have been akin to residing at the bottom of the runway. Perhaps Milton Keynes would have become a replica of Crawley to the south of Gatwick. Instead of a multi-industry city, Milton Keynes would have been almost entirely dependent upon the airport for its employment. It is estimated that fifty thousand people would have worked at the airport.

It was the most efficiently organised public protest since the anti-coral Corn Law League of 1839. The outward manifestation was a host of signs reading NO

AIRPORT HERE. They sprang up overnight along roads and adjacent to the railway between Bletchley and Leighton Buzzard. But the organisation went much deeper than that.

The Wing Airport Resistance Association was under the chairmanship of Desmond Fennell, later to be Justice Fennel and head that Kings Cross enquiry and Evelyn de Rothschild from the family of merchant bankers as treasurer. The local population banded together to prevent at all costs an airport being built on their doorstep. Many other famous names like Johnny Dankworth, Cleo Lane and Roald Dahl, who all lived in the area, threw in their unqualified support. (Robert Maxwell, millionaire publisher and MP joined in but history now shows that his motives and intentions were decidedly unclear.)

They knew only too well they had an uphill task ahead of them for in every way Cubblington/Wing was the best site for the airport. Had it come to North Buckinghamshire, London Milton Keynes International Airport may not have become London's third airport at all but the countries first airport ! There would have been no need than for Luton, Birmingham or even East Midlands airports and much of the traffic would have been stolen away from Heathrow.

I recently spent a pleasant evening with WARA executive committee member Dennis Skinner in his Whitchurch home, enjoying his hospitality about a roaring log fire as he explained the airport perimeter fence had been planned for no more than one hundred yards away from where we were sitting. It is his belief that Milton Keynes would have needed to expand south to meet the airport, swallowing up everything as far as Leighton Buzzard. The resulting conurbation, some planners saw it reaching right down to Aylesbury, would be little like the city we know today.

On another evening I chatted with Farmer Morris and his wife from Manor Farm, Hoggeston realising we were right in the middle of where the main runway would have been. Their family has farmed land in the village for ten generations dating back to the 1700's. What a personal tragedy it would have been to fall victim to a compulsory purchase order.

Eighty year old Rector of Dunton, the Reverend Hubert Sillitoe, brother of Sir Percy Sillitoe head of wartime MI5, preached hell, fire and damnation against all airport planners. He was a popular character, if a little eccentric, and achieved fame in The Sun newspaper who dubbed him a modern-day Elijah. They quoted one of his speeches ... *This damn sacrilege we will fight on the door steps of our homes, in the fields of our farms, at churchyard gates and church doors !* A later edition of the paper had on its front page a picture of this campaigning cleric setting fire to a giant copy of the government's report and reprinting his prayer *...that these inhuman and sacrilegious proposals be so absolutely rejected and reduced the flames of fire shall reduce this copy of the Roskill Report.* The reporter went on to describe how the flames leaped upwards as a brass band played the funeral march. But others attracted less favourable media attention. There were those who thought the best thing to do would be to load up their tractors with manure and dump the lot on Downing Street. Mr Justice Roskill, detailed by Harold Wilson's government to study the various sites for the airport, actually received death threats. Some of the protest posters and cartoons in the national press made no secret of the intention many had of actually turning the campaign into a literal fight if talking failed !

I asked Mr Morris if he thought people would have really engaged in hand to hand fighting with bulldozers. A mild mannered man himself, he doubted if he would have actually been involved but was certain others would. WARA not only had to tackle the politicians and bureaucrats but also had to disassociate themselves from any threats of violent activity activities if they were to maintain credibility.

The membership of Robert Maxwell was also hardly an asset to the group. Maxwell, as recent events now only to clearly show, was a past master when it came to playing one person off against another. He played WARA off against his own political party and the local community against the planners but never failed to keep his own business interests uppermost. It was reported in the Guardian on 15th June 1970 that Maxwell said to a Bletchley factory worker *Let's get Milton Keynes first if we can have the airport as well so much the better !*

Three days later he lost his seat to Bill Benyon, so ending his parliamentary career, and he subsequently left the executive committee of WARA.

Dennis Skinner is convinced it was the election of a Conservative Government, under Prime Minister Ted Heath, that finally saved the day. Wing was the best, but also the most expensive option, in his opinion the Wilson Government had little regard for the costs. Tories, on the other hand, weighed finances with rather more care and eventually went for the cheaper Stanstead project.

WARA attacked the finances of the proposal on every front. It strived all along to avoid becoming a political body, something that frustrated Robert Maxwell, but to truly represent everyone who was against the airport. This included Buckinghamshire County Council, Milton Keynes Development Corporation and just about every living soul within twenty miles of the proposed airport. There was little to be gained by stressing the environmental issues which carried no weight in the swinging sixties. Instead the organisation employed professionals to undertake their own investigations then question every facet of the government's Roskill Report.

Their arguments were presented to every member of parliament whose final decision found against Wing. While that managed to convince them but the costing was wrong, indeed it was. Nearly a quarter of a century later it has become clear that a London Milton Keynes International Airport, as well as handling more than its fair share of business and cargo traffic, would have developed into the nation's number one holiday resort.

Nobody in the 1960's quite foresaw such an explosion in leisure travel.

There was a victory torchlight procession from Stewkley Church on 26th April 1971, a tree planted in the churchyard at Whitchurch proclaims: *This tree is planted to the glory of God and in thankfulness for having been spared the third London airport 26th of November 1972.* Buckinghamshire County Council planted the spinney at Cubblington upon the site originally intended for the terminal building.

Little now remains of the actual project, the signs have been taken down, the graffiti that once adorned motorway bridges have been sponged off but in the barn at Manor Farm where many of the rallies were held there is still a mural demanding NO AIRPORT. When I saw it a couple of weeks ago a herd of beef cattle ambled about in their winter quarters oblivious of the fact that they could have been jumbo jets.

But would Milton Keynes be a better place at double its size and serving one of the world's major airports ? Perhaps, perhaps not. It is difficult to say. During the campaign the activities of WARA cannot have escaped the notice of teenager Richard Branson, then a border at Stowe School near Buckingham. Would it be better if Virgin Atlantic, together with British Airways, American Airlines and all the rest, brought their vast needs for employment to the area ?

Next time you are sitting in the traffic on the M25 as you head off on holiday by way of Heathrow or Gatwick you can weigh up the advantages and disadvantages then decide yourself.

MILTON KEYNES HOSPITAL ACTION GROUP:
Marlborough Street, the V8, was the first major grid road to be set down within the New City of Milton Keynes. To its west now stands Milton Keynes General Hospital. But it hasn't always been like that.

I wonder if the good citizens of Milton Keynes realise just how fortunate they are in the city's hospital and what a first class job the trustees are currently doing in managing it on our behalf.

Most people, I suppose, hold the medical profession in high esteem, and quite rightly so. But too often they are forced to do their work within the frustrating, even conflicting, bureaucracy of the National Health Service. But to me, an ordinary customer of the NHS, it would appear that in Milton Keynes all concerned have the chemistry right in order to serve the public.

Recently one of my children was admitted to Ward 18 by the Accident and Emergency Department, spending three days in the hospital and having a minor operation. I have to say I could not have been more favourably impressed with every aspect of the work I encountered.

Not only were all the staff incredibly kind and patient but the entire hospital seemed to be so very well run. It presented an atmosphere of spacious, airy and clean environment. Wide ranging facilities for patients and visitors and a medical team infusing confidence. The food in the Eaglestone Rooms, open to visitors, could rival any in Milton Keynes and certainly beat all comers on pricing. Many major retailers would do well by taking notes of the shopping facilities in the entrance foyer and the BBC could learn a thing or two by listening to the Hospital Radio.

I have seen a lot of some of the major teaching hospitals in this country and I can tell you many of them could not stand alongside our hospital. Don't take this the wrong way but it's almost worth being ill just to be there !

But things have not always being like this. In the early days of the city the nearest hospital was a thirty mile drive away at Stoke Mandeville in Aylesbury. It is a certain fact that people suffered, even died, because they could not obtain specialist medical treatment quickly enough. I watched, in 1975, as a young man died of a heart attack while it took forty minutes to get him to a doctor .

Events like this gave fuel to a rapidly growing pressure in the shape of the Milton Keynes Hospital Action Group . Its members lobbied parliament, local authorities and the Development Corporation with the full weight of public opinion behind them. Their campaign slogan Milton Keynes Is Dying For A Hospital was turned into car stickers and adorned the rear windows of hundreds throughout the city.

A giant orange question mark was sculptured and erected in the field designated for the hospital site.

It was a very special day for all when the first sod was turned in the hospital's construction. Happily, along with those car stickers, slogans and question mark are gone as are the days when a drive to hospital meant a thirty minute dash to Aylesbury or Northampton.

So on behalf of those in Milton Keynes who would wish to associate themselves with these comments, I acknowledge the grand job being done by doctors, nurses, caterers, domestic staff, managers and all at Milton Keynes Hospital Action Group . Thanks to all for giving us a hospital to be proud of.

Oh And By The Way:
Every Sunday morning something like three thousand people flock to the hospital car boot sale where anything up to two hundred stalls sell a wider variety of antiques, curio's, object d'art and more plain ordinary junk than was ever found in the Portobello Road during its heyday.

In recent years the car boot sale has become an addition to the British way of life with Milton Keynes getting in on the ground floor. Now managed by one of the country's largest market operators under licence from the trustees the hospital boot sale was one of the first in the country to begin regular trading.

All this brought in a valuable source of income for our hospital at the same time providing a measure of innocent fun to all comers. If you have never been along to the sale, drop by next Sunday but be prepared to haggle for the bargains in MK's version of the Kaili Bazzaz - The Old Bazaar In Cairo !

A thirty year update – We ARE The Concrete Cows: Milton Keynes General Hospital is now University Hospital Milton Keynes. How proud I am sure all Milton Keynes Hospital Action Group members would be seeing just how special is the hospital our city is blessed with.

However, where the car boot sale once happened is a giant car park with hideous rip off charges. NHS – free at the point of delivery ? Not if you have to park your car !

QUEENSWAY – NO LONGER FIT FOR A QUEEN: Before the days of Milton Keynes it had always been known as Bletchley Road but a visit in the late 1960's by Queen Elizabeth II re-christened the town shopping street to Queensway. There used to be a sign commemorating the visit but this has now disappeared and with it the street of twenty-five years ago to be replaced with something quite different.

Queensway begins where the Buckingham Road passes beneath the railway bridge carrying the mainline south to London. Its continuity is at present broken by the Brunel Centre and Bletchley Market but it originally stretched in one length to Fenny Stratford.
As a matter of interest the train line has not always being carried by a bridge. Where the road now dips down to pass beneath the railway there used to be a level crossing. It was a petition by the Reverend

Broughton, Rector of Bletchley between 1832 and 1861, that forced the excavation and lowering the road to its present level. Sir Herbert Leon, of Bletchley Park, erected a horse trough for the animals to drink from after climbing the newly shaped hill towards the station but that is another story.

More than a hundred years later other excavations began to change again the contour of the area. After driving beneath the bridge the travellers passed the Park Hotel on the right at the junction with Duncombe Street then Lloyds Bank and Cowley and Wilson's Garage. Fronting the left-hand side were Barclays Bank, Greens Newsagents an assortment of shops belonging to the Co-op.

For day after day in the in 1972 the dull thump of a pie hammer could be heard throughout the area as a huge steel retaining girders were forced into ground to hold up the railway embankments, allowing the cutting away the slope at the building of Saxon Street. This was needed as Queensway was to be closed to traffic from Duncombe Street to Albert Street. With the new road open, demolition work began on Cowling Wilson's Garage whose business was relocated in Aylesbury Street, Fenny Stratford. Upon its former site excavation work began to build the walkway into the new Brunel Centre. Something of a major attraction among the morning shoppers one day was a giant excavator crane upside down in the hole it had previously dug. The unfortunate driver had forgotten to put out the stabilisers before starting work and the machine had simply toppled in.

Also demolished were Greens Newsagents, which moved into the Brunel Centre on the site of the now Martins, and the various Co-op shops whose management took advantage of the development to build their Stanier House department store.

Many of the familiar shops of the early 1970's, those days of the infant New City, have since disappeared. Gone are Pollard's Hardware, Marshalls music shop, Fine Fare Supermarket and Woolworths which once stood opposite the market.

It was locating Bletchley Market in the middle of Queensway that broke its length for a second time. The architecture of the area was severely criticised on the day it went up and it has never been popular with the local people ever since.

One of the Queensway's landmarks to have changed, although not to have completely disappeared, is the Northampton and Midland Building Society with its charismatic manager who was heavily involved in a wide range of community activities. Financial mergers saw it join forces with the Anglia then later to become Anglia Hastings and Thanet Building Society. Quite a mouthful, so Anglia became its new name. But not for long, another merger gave us the Nationwide Anglia before revising to Nationwide with offices at 99 Queensway. The original Northampton and Midland offices at 239 Queensway is now Knights Pharmacy.

The coming of the Point in Central Milton Keynes caused Bletchley to lose its last remaining cinema, The Studio, which used to be where Studio Court is now. But it was the closing and demolition of Queens Swimming Pool, under the former Labour controlled Bletchley Urban District Council, that caused the greatest public outcry. The pool, the factory of Bletchley Printers and Central Gardens were all to go to make way for a new leisure centre. Folk were pleased enough to look forward to the brand new sporting facilities the centre would bring the town but they were far from happy to see their swimming bath be replaced with a leisure pool complete with palm trees and plastic dolphins ! The council had its way in the end but recreation committee chairman, Ron Staniford, paid the price by losing his seat in the next election.

Queensway is probably now the least fashionable shopping centre in the whole of Milton Keynes and is in danger, within future decades, of becoming something of a ghost town as patrons desert it for the more comfortable environment to be found about the city.

In the one hundred years preceding the arrival of Milton Keynes Development Corporation Queensway reached out from Bletchley to Fenny Stratford to become a popular collection of retail shops. But the apparent haphazard planning during the latter part of this century has brought it to his present sorry state.

For example, whoever designed the Brunel Centre ? Who could possibly have conceived shops about a dark tunnel with no natural light and totally inadequate artificial illuminations ? The centre directory, unchanged since opening, points shoppers enigmatically to John Walton, John Collier (Remember the famous window to watch ?) and Peter Lord - all long since defunct !

Queensway is the only High Street in the area not to celebrate Christmas with lights and decorations. Why is that ?

Was proper thought ever given to car parking ? Who is sensibly going to pay for the privilege of shopping at Sainsbury's, having also to leave a deposit on the trolley, when just down the road on Watling Street Tesco cheerfully offers both parking and use of shopping trolleys entirely free of charge ?

In a city of trees why are those in Queensbury so decrepit no self-respecting dog would ever cock its leg against them. Did the landscape gardeners never find their way that far south ?

At the outset of Milton Keynes Development Corporation there were many grand plans and ideas for the area. Whatever became of them ?

The new owners of Brunel Shopping Centre, London an Associate Investment Trust, is currently unveiling proposals to refurbish this design folly of Bletchley. But until somebody also takes a grip on the remainder of the deteriorating situation perhaps Queensway is better left to the memories of those now pre Development Corporation days !

EDUCATION – A GIFT FOR LIFE – AND MORE

I while ago I saw a sticker on the back window of a car which boldly stated IF YOU CAN READ THIS THEN THANK A TEACHER.

How very true that statement is: *If you can read this then thank a teacher.* Without the ability to read we writers would soon be out of a job as would all newspaper and book publishers, the likes of WH Smith and John Menzies would join the dole queue and we may as well all go back to living in caves wearing animal skins and hunting with clubs.

Sixty years ago schools throughout the area held a special celebration to commemorate education over the past one hundred years. Souvenir programmes were printed, children had special lessons, concerts were given and a number of educational visits were organised. But education in Milton Keynes dates back much, much further than then. (Remember this text comes from Not The Concrete Cows published in 1994.)

There is a record of a Chantry Chapel being built onto the church in Bletchley in the early 1300's and part of the Chantry Priest's business was as keeper of a free school for the poor of the parish.

In 1388 at the Manor Court held in Fenny Stratford a William Barton claimed that he was owed eighteen pence (Seven and a half pence in today's money) for services as a teacher. The debt was upheld and ordered to be settled in full.

After the War of the Roses education in North Buckinghamshire began to significantly develop. There is an entry in the Bletchley registrar dated 15th May 1587 recording the marriage of William de Schoolam of Bletchley to Joan Pennington. William taught at the school supported by the lord of the manor.

Seven years earlier a school had been established in the North Chapel of Milton Keynes Church, the teacher had to supplement his income by working as the village sieve maker. And teachers today think they are hard done by !

Lands near to Buckingham were rented out in 1423 at thirteen shillings and four pence per year for used by a grammar school. The exact location is uncertain but possibly the school was at Thornton. Initially it had just six students. In 1574 the endowment the school was receiving from the lord of the manor, Roberts Ingleton, was transferred to the Royal Latin School at Buckingham. That particular school, of course, is still very much in existence today.

Doctor John Radcliffe, who died in 1714, left in his will a great deal of property to University College Oxford for funding medical training. Radcliffe Observatory and Library in Oxford also owe their initial existence to his generosity. In addition, the good doctor financed the enlarging of Saint Bartholomew's Hospital in London. The Radcliffe School in Wolverton takes its name from this particular philanthropic doctor.
The Reverend W Cole recorded in 1712 that twenty children in the Bletchley and Fenny Stratford area were being taught in the charge of the church.

In a list of chantry schools within Buckinghamshire, published in 1720, a school is stated to have been erected in Bletchley although the exact location is uncertain.

A few years later Doctor Brown Willis maintained at his own expense schools in Bletchley, Fenny Stratford and in Whaddon.

On the 10th October 1726 there was held the first meeting at Newport Pagnell of a society to promote education among the poor of the Newport Hundreds.

Within the coming of the industrial revolution, putting the area on main routes of road, rail and canal, another significance forward step was taken. October 1811 saw the foundation of the National Society for Educating in the Church. This society contributed, in 1815, the sum of thirty pounds towards building a school in Fenny Stratford. This was then maintained by the local clergy. In 1819 there were one hundred and seven pupils on the roll with the Mr Webb as headmaster. He was paid the princely sum of fifty pounds a year as his salary.

In 1838 the Bletchley School united to the National Society. In 1840 land was acquired to build a new school. This was sold by Sir Philip Duncombe, 1st Baronet of Great Brickhill, to the Rector and Church Wardens for just five shillings. (25p in today's money.) The school stood on Watling Street near to Fenny Stratford Railway Station.

In 1887 the premises were transferred to a school board and 204 students were recorded on roll.

The Fenny Stratford School Board was due to open for business during the last week of August 1887 but was delayed until 12th September due to an outbreak of typhoid fever in the area. The headmaster of the day recorded the epidemic in the school logbook but did not note down how many children were taken ill or indeed died.

Local legend has it that this new school building was cited upon a plague pit dating from the middle ages.

Records of schools in the south of the area are still in existence and give a full picture of all that went on. The curriculum at best in the late in nineteenth century can be described as *thin*. The logbook records all the poems and songs that children knew but pays little attention to mathematics, reading and writing.

Official reports over the next few years criticised the standards and there is a note of at least one teacher being dismissed for failing to bring children up to the expected test levels.

In the north of the area, however, standards were thriving. In Wolverton the directors of the railway took a keen interest in the schooling of all local children, seeing it as an investment to provide for a well-educated future workforce.

Is September 1847 the directors report stated: The school, which is very near to the works, is surrounded by a small court and garden. In the centre is a room for girls from 5 to 9 years of age who are instructed by a governess in reading, writing, arithmetic, geography, grammar, history and needlework. Here we counted fifty-five clean healthy faces. In the east wing there were ninety-five stout, athletic boys of various ages learning mathematics and drawing, including quadratic equations, euclid, land surveying, trigonometry and even conic sections.

Despite the high proportion of Milton Keynes children educated today within private schools no traditional public schools were established in our area like of Bedford to the east and Eton to the south.

The Rev W T Sankey became vicar of St Giles, Stony Stratford, in 1859 and founded Saint Paul's School in the town. It cost a staggering £40,000 opening with two hundred boys and very soon established a sound reputation producing many distinguished pupils.

The boys followed a strict routine with morning roll call at 5:45am ! Work began immediately with breakfast not until 8:30am. Tuition continued until lunchtime with games during the afternoon. Lessons then were held in the evening from 6:00pm to 8:30pm. Prefects had the power to fag younger boys and corporal punishment was in daily use. When Sankey died these were taken to excess and the school declined. It eventually closed in 1895.

Another private school in Stony Stratford was run between 1840 and 1870 on the corner of Market Square and Mill Lane by Joseph Hambling. Charles Dickens met him on one visit to the area and based the character of Mr Turveydrop in Bleak House upon him.

Bletchley Conservative Club in Queensway may also have begun its life as a private school.

Sir Herbert Leon and his young wife Fanny came to Bletchley in 1882 and busied themselves in every aspect of local affairs. Although the Leons educated their own sons at Eton they became increasingly involved in the Bletchley Schools. Their later years coincided with the appointment of Ernest Cook as headmaster and education in Bletchley thrived.

In recognition of their efforts Headmaster David Bradshaw and his board of governors changed the name of Bletchley School to Leon School. Although the new buildings were erected in the south of the town in the early 1970's the school retains the name.
Ernest Cooke retired at the end of summer term in 1953 after twenty-nine years service. His contribution to education in the south of the city had been tremendous and long lasting.

Harold Wilson's Labour Government of the 1960's introduced comprehensive education to the nation. Although the rest of Buckinghamshire retained grammar schools the socialist councils within the New City managed to turn the area's schools into the non-selective comprehensive style. They appeared to work very well but the debate and demand for grammar school refuses to go away. As a result, private education in Milton Keynes currently thrives.

A MAN WHO GIVES YOU MONEY GIVES YOU NOTHING BUT A MAN WHO GIVES YOU HIS TIME GIVES YOU HIS LIFE

That sounds a bit profound doesn't it? The kind of thing that may have been said by Voltaire or Gandhi. The truth is that it is only a humble quote from Yours Truly.

It fascinates me, and indeed somewhat moves me, how quite ordinary people are prepared to give freely of their time to help others. Milton Keynes is full of scout leaders, carers, church workers and a whole army of those who invest their time in others. Without them it would be a much poorer place.

To do correct justice to all the voluntary organisations in the area we would need a book of its own but over 1993 and 1994 I featured three in the Milton Keynes Citizen which I pleased to here to bring to your attention again. To one I have added text on something I wrote for a leading national magazine. My reasons for doing so will become clear as you read it.

LIGHTFORCE INTERNATIONAL – A LIGHT IN THE DARKNESS:

Twelve months ago walking into the hospital, nestling in the snow-capped mountains of Northern Albania, was like entering a nightmare of gargantuan proportions.

Upon urine soiled beds were patients in danger of the most petty ailments turning into terminal illnesses. The maternity ward had no proper water supply and babies were being delivered with little medical support upon nothing more than a folding camp bed. The same razor blade was being used to cut the umbilical cord of every child without any means to antiseptically cleanse it between patients. The chance, therefore, of healthy survival for these babies was, at the very best, slender.

Today things are different. Instead of cockroaches there is an air of cleanliness and hygiene, instead of battered and rusting cots there are modern beds and instead of cracked wash basins there are modern bathrooms. All of this thanks to the efforts of one hundred and fifty volunteers, tons of relief aid and hours upon hours of backbreaking hard work.

Albania is three days hard driving from England and yet to the five hundred strong congregation of the Milton Keynes Christian Centre on Oldbrook it is just around the corner.

It was the most prolific of or Biblical writers, Saint Paul, who declared that faith divorce from deed is barren. Possibly one of the most successful churches in the country, The Christian and its congregation organise a one hundred place day nursery, book shop, children's programmes, cafeteria, accommodation for the homeless and a worldwide outreach. But here outreach does not just mean putting money onto a collection plate, it means sending members out to actually do the work. Perhaps this attitude of putting faith firmly into action is, in itself, the underlying reason behind the church's phenomenal success .

Their first ever relief mission took place in late 1984 sending a five ton truck out behind the Iron Curtain and into Poland. (Today Poland sends out its own relief missions.) With the downfall of Ceausescu a party from the Milton Keynes Christian Centre was among the first western agencies to enter Romania. Over the next two years many visits were made from the church to the town Arad near to the Hungarian border.

With relief work now formalised as Lightforce International full time workers from the church are maintained in Mongolia, Hungary, the former Yugoslavia, the Crimea, Moldova and Albania.

The Bosnian conflict and the road inaccessibility of Albania have made it difficult for Western Europeans to appreciate the desperate need a country where 65% of the population live in remote mountain villages and where conditions would have been archaic in mediaeval times. But when the plight of this pitiful nation county came to the attention of senior pastor and Lightforce director George Ridley the church threw itself wholeheartedly behind the provision of relief .

During 1993 one hundred and fifty volunteers paid their own way to Albania, transporting more than fifty tons of aid, working in twelve separate villages, helping a staggering eight thousand people and totally renovating the Lure Hospital.

The medical director wrote to Milton Keynes saying: *We thank you for your great job repairing the hospital, fixing the bathrooms, giving us other equipment such as a sink, showers etc and for bringing the toilets up to European standards.*

But plans for 1994 are even more ambitious. Five hundred workers, from teenagers to grandparents, will each spent two weeks in forty separate remote towns and villages many of which can only be reached by four wheel drive vehicles. It is intended to re-roof a school and totally renovate for a four storey hospital. Fourteen coaches have been chartered to ferry the volunteers to and from England.

The relief is being coordinated by former Royal Engineer Tim Miles and has the first party organised to leave Milton Keynes on the 28th April.

Those who have already given of their time to work in the mission recognise how much it has changed their lives. Said Christine Topham: *Albania has been a life changing experience and opened my eyes to many things. I'll never complain about English rain again !*

Siobhan Malone from Oldbrook added: *Never again shall I take a fresh flushable toilet and warm water for granted ! It has been a God-given experience full of wonder, amazement and learning.*

Dave Malloy offered advice to future volunteers: *Come prepared to share your skills, be willing to do anything and be open to learn.*

Yet it is staggering that this tremendous undertaking is going on without the knowledge of most of us in the city. Can modesty be taken so far ? In the same way that Albania failed to attract the attention of the national media, as did Romania and East Germany, so Milton Keynes has taken little notice of the work on Oldbrook. Not only should we applaud the efforts of these good people but many of us perhaps wish to join in.

Lightforce director George Ridley explained that while they are no longer looking for volunteers for the coming season the charity will be willing to interview anyone with a burning desire to travel with one of the relief parties. Neither are they in need of bin bags of clothing, it cost £25 and ship out each sack of relief goods.

So what, I asked, do you need ? How could the citizens of Milton Keynes help ? George smiled and handed me a shopping list first aid equipment and medical supplies putty, paint an fillers brushes, rollers and plaster sanitary ware, tiles and plumbing equipment, roofing materials, ladders, wheelbarrows cement mixers, and generators.
If someone would like to offer another Land Rover, he added, we wouldn't say no !

While all volunteers pay their own way to and from the relief area, costing anything up to £500, the project has to provide the food for its workers. So if anyone has enough cornflakes kicking about to feed five hundred people for two weeks of breakfast the hungry volunteers will be pleased to take them off your hands.

Wanting to know more or offer assistance you are invited to contact George Ridley director of Lightforce International at the Milton Keynes Christian Centre.

Lightforce is a long-term project so even if you are reading this book many years after its initial publication the work will still be going on.

Thirty years later – We ARE The Concrete Cows:
Lightforce is still operational. Still operational in Albania as well as working in Uganda and India.

Working as a freelance feature writer for the local paper I have come to meet some very interesting people and I have been fascinated by their activities. When I spent some time with Valley Medical Transport to write about their life-giving service I ended up being invited onto their board of trustees. Let me first of all introduce you to their work with my original feature after which I will bring you a little up to date on the charity's activities. Valley Medical Transport, a friend to all.

VALLEY MEDICAL TRANSPORT – A FRIEND TO ALL:
If you look into your car mirror and see a silver Vauxhall Carlton, equipped with blue flashing lights, get out of the driver's way he will be on a vital mission of mercy.

Milton Keynes based, Valley Medical Transport grew originally after one man's interest and desire to support transplant surgery. Now poised to become a fully registered charity, this organisation aims be on call twenty-four hours a day to both patients and doctors throughout the region.

When a donor organ is found the area transplant co-ordinator is faced with dozens of tasks all of which have to come together with a degree of precision and within a strictly framed timetable. A team of surgeons has to be dispatched to harvest the organ from its donor, on many occasions several teams are needed depending on the number of organs suitable for transplant. (This can include the heart, lungs, liver, kidneys, pancreas and corneas.) The recipient has to be alerted and admitted to hospital, the transplant team called and made ready and, of course, the organs themselves transported, sometimes many hundreds of miles from donor to recipient hospitals.

Various options are available to transplant the organs, but none of them without associated significant costs. A commercial express courier service is likely to run into several hundreds of pounds, one hospital recently paid a staggering £3.50p a mile to move a pancreas from the North of England to the Home Counties ! An alternative could be the ambulance service but that would tie up a high tech vehicle together with highly trained crew who strictly speaking should be out saving lives. Again there is a charge and, in these days of interdepartmental billing, the recipient hospital will be fully invoiced for the costs involved.

Using a registered ambulance vehicle and advising police forces of its movements within their areas, Valley Medical Transport can provide a highly efficient and professional method of moving organs at a fraction of the commercial cost. Already on call to the Churchill Hospital in Oxford and the Royal Free Hospital in London the organisation is now looking to extend its services to many other centres.

Although Milton Keynes is not a transplant centre Valley Medical Transport offers help to the team of surgeons sent out to collect the donated organ. *At the time such as this, when the surgeon is mentally preparing himself for the operation*, explained a spokesman, *it is hardly fair to expect him to have to drive a long distance to a strange hospital, negotiating traffic along the way, and then when he has the organ to have to drive it back. We will chauffeur him both ways, relieving much of the stress and leaving him only to have to do the job for which he has been most expertly trained.* Once certain formalities have been concluded Valley Medical will be providing this service to surgeons within a group of London transplant centres and should be starting work next month.

The third arm of the service is designed to support the patient. When the prospective patient is placed on call for an organ their life is initially dominated by the telephone. Every time it rings their heart misses a beat in anticipation. But a patient can be on call for many months, years even, before a suitable organ is found so after a few weeks this tends to fade and take a background place and, while not forgotten, it certainly no longer governs every minute of their day. When the long-awaited call eventually does come the patient and their family are no longer fully prepared in quite the same way as they were on day one and consequently often thrown into chaos.

David Ashford, who hopes shortly to be joining the board of trustees and whose ten year old daughter, Rebekah, has been through two transplants explained: *On both occasions the first thing to do was to fill the car with petrol, of course we should have kept the tank topped up but just as it ran low we were called. Then came the problem of finding a working cash machine, not the easiest of tasks on earth. Once all the dashing about was over and the suitcase hastily packed we began to seventy-five mile drive to the hospital. With just about every emotion imaginable crashing through our minds cover I have to question just how fit I was mentally to sit behind the wheel.*

Valley Medical Transport will put itself on call together with the patient, being ready night or day to handle all transport arrangements currently free of charge. Guys Hospital, which performs somewhere in the order of one hundred kidney transplants a year has put the organisation on standby for its paediatric patients and will shortly be adding in many of its adult patients. Of these there is a young baby living in the West of Ireland, when his call comes Valley Medical will be waiting at Heathrow Airport to meet the plane.

There are currently nearly five thousand patients in Great Britain waiting for transplants, such operations of which cost many thousands of pounds carefully juggled within tightly controlled budgets. This newly formed charity aims to save hospitals anything up to 75% on the on their transport costs so freeing much needed finance for treatment.

Although Milton Keynes itself is nowhere to be found on the medical transplant map Valley Medical Transport and its board of trustees aim to put the city firmly in the centre of what they hoping in time to come will become a nationwide service supporting patients and hospital doctors in this life giving field.

Any patient in Milton Keynes already on call for an organ transplant is invited to contact Valley Medical Transport to find out how the transport programme could possibly help them.

That was how my report appeared in the Milton Keynes Citizen in August 1993 . Valley Medical Transport went on to achieve full registration with the charity commissioners and is currently on call to most transplant centres in the region. The baby from Ireland did receive his transplant Valley Medical was there waiting at Heathrow for him. Let me tell you now about that story.

It was a filthy night. The wind was battering the side of our house and the rain hitting the ground so hard it was bouncing up again for several inches. I hate winter afternoons when it becomes prematurely dark, on this day it felt as if it had been dark since lunchtime. I had gone out in the car to meet my son's school bus and saving the drenching walking home would have given him.

As I pulled up in front of my home my wife was standing there waiting to meet me. "Valley Medical just phoned, can you go with the driver to Heathrow Airport ? There's a baby being flown in from Ireland for a transplant in London."

A quick snatch for my camera notebook and money before I too was standing in the driveway waiting for the car. I heard the sirens well before it pulled up, it's blue flashing lights illuminating the entire street. A night of high drama was about to unfold.

London Heathrow is not the most accessible place on earth and hardly user friendly. On a stormy night with extensive roadworks on the M1 it was going to be difficult, It was the time when the extra lane was being added to the section between Luton and the A5 junctions with the contractors thinking it would be fun to close most of the access points onto the motorway.

The kidney is an organ that will tolerate being out of the body for quite some time but the shorter the period between donor and recipient the better.

The identity of the donor is kept strictly confidential so this particular organ could have come from anywhere in the country, indeed anywhere in Northern Europe. There is no way we could know the time scale involved but we did know that Valley Medical had been charged with getting the patient from the airport to the hospital as quickly as possible.

With the frustration of the motorway roadworks we decided to opt for the A5. My job was to sit in the passenger seat and work the siren, leaving the driver to concentrate fully on the road. I have to confess a certain thrill and sense of power as I flicked the switch screaming the cars ahead of us after the way. It was a terrific responsibility, not only was it important we get through as quickly as possible but safety had to be preserved not only for ourselves but also for every other road user.

The charity's office had faxed all police forces along our route to advise them of our movements. On the M25 officers in a police Range Rover waved and gave us thumbs up as we passed.

The weather was steadily worsening with gales battering the car. A severe weather warning was in force and we could not help thinking about our infant charge high over the Irish Sea. What kind of a flight was he having ?

At Terminal One the police were waiting for us and directed us to a reserved parking place right outside the Aer Lingus gate. It was the first time I have never had any difficulty parking at Heathrow !

Inside Aer Lingus staff were trying hard to cope with the worst night for flying all year. Many aircraft had been unable to take off from the smaller Irish airfields and our Dublin flight had been delayed. There was nothing we could do but wait.

The airline staff were brilliant. The patient was highlighted on the passenger computer and a special escort detailed to meet him and his mother once the plane was on the ground. Heathrow's police liaised with customs and immigration to ensure no delay but first the aircraft had to land.

I am afraid I may have made myself something of a nuisance as I pestered the Aer Lingus staff for updates on the aircraft's progress.

It's just 20 minutes away Sir.

Is holding in the stack, shouldn't be too long now.

Then, just as we were about to suggest we ask air traffic control to run up a ladder and bring everybody down, came the news we wanted. *They're on final approach now.*

The aircraft on the ground now. Shouldn't be much longer. Eventually young Jamie and his mum excitedly emerged. Into the car and we were off towards London on the M4.

It was two weeks before Christmas and the lights of Harrods shone more brightly than those of our car. We covered the distance from the airport to Guys Hospital in just half an hour delivering young Jamie in time for his transplant. Another successful mission for Milton Keynes based Valley Medical Transport.

The next week Valley Medical's Vauxhall Carlton went underwent a transplant of its own. Although the car is always maintained in perfect order its engine was gaining in mileage and, with over 100,000 miles on the clock was not going to go on for ever.

First of all Vauxhall Motors in Luton offered a brand new engine free of charge then Milton Keynes Cowley and Wilson generously offered to fit it, performing a heart transplant on the car, entirely free of charge. It's new engine beating beneath the bonnet, the car is back on the road performing its duties whenever the call goes out for help.

A LADY WITH A SPECIAL MISSION:

My own daughter has suffered from renal failure since she was three years old and so my interest in the donor card programme is deeply personal. After a third attempt at a kidney transplant in London's Guys Hospital I was offered an interview with Mrs Elizabeth Ward, president of the British Kidney Patients Association, in order to prepare a feature for national magazine.

By her own admission Mrs Ward is a formidable lady and so I have to admit to a certain sense of apprehension as I prepared for our meeting. When the brief meeting was over my whole being resounded with shell shock. Rather than my interviewing her, Mrs Ward had clearly interviewed me and I'm not sure if I passed the test or not ! However, it was that strong personality which was directly responsible for the introduction of our familiar donor card.

Outwardly Nigel and Elizabeth Ward have everything in the world: a lovely house overlooking rolling countryside, a successful business, holidays abroad, a full social life and three wonderful children. It was as their son Timothy, affectionately known as Timbo, was about to enter Harrow School that the family had to cope with the devastating news he was suffering from a life threatening kidney disorder.

As one who has had to accept the same reality, I can empathise with Timbo's parents but in 1994 medical science has come a very long way from when the Ward Family had to cope with their situation. Then funding for renal dialysis provided but a few machines and organ transplantation was in its infancy. It looked as if Timbo did not have a very long life ahead of him.

Timbo attended school with the son of Sir Keith Joseph, then Minister of Health. When Elizabeth was sent a kidney donor card in use in the United States she began campaigning for a similar system to be introduced in Great Britain. She wrote many times to Sir Keith, at first suggesting, then urging and finally bullying him towards the introduction of a kidney donor card.

The first renal transplants had been performed in Boston, Massachusetts, as far back as 1954. Ten years later the first operation was attempted in this country. But without a supply of organs there was little future in transplant surgery.

In 1967 world attention unfortunately focused on South Africa where Christian Barnard performed the first human heart transplant on a 54 year old patient. The surrounding media circus, failure rate and questioning of the ethics involved in such programmes did little to prepare public opinion for transplant donor card.

There were those who found the idea of spare part surgery repulsive, almost akin to cannibalism, while others feared the removal of organs before the donor was honestly dead. Ignorance and prejudice ruled over medical science.

Eventually Sir Keith Joseph agreed to discuss Mrs Ward's proposals and a card based on her own design was launched in 1971 as the kidney donor card. I remember the one I carried from the early 1970's, I must still have it somewhere, having to ask my father, as next of kin, to sign his agreement on it. Like many relatives of the time he was reluctant to agree. For others the reluctance became outright refusal.

A change of government saw Barbara Castle and Doctor David Owen at the Department of Health. The redoubtable Mrs Ward confronted them and the realisation that her husband could refuse legal permission for her to become a donor appalled Mrs Castle suffragette instincts. She demanded the condition be removed.

The next twenty years saw not only transplants being accepted as by far the best treatment for chronic renal failure but also the successful grafting of hearts, liver, cornea and more recently the spleen. To meet the widening of science health minister Doctor Gerard Vaughn oversaw the kidney donor card's transformation into the organ donor card.

But this was a change the campaigning Mrs Ward did not exactly welcome. "The indelicate wording of the card makes it look like a butcher shopping list !" She complained to me in the sitting room of her Surrey home and the headquarters of the British Kidney Patients Association. "And the widening of the scope most certainly denies in many cases the use of donor kidneys."

Unlike the heart and liver the kidney is a resilient organ, it can survive for several hours outside the body and can be removed quite successfully for transplant after the heart has stopped beating. Mrs Ward went on to explain how this enabled relatives to say a proper and dignified goodbye to their loved ones whereas now donors bodies have to be clinically kept alive on a machine while the brain is dead and the soul departed.

Consistent high profile over more than two decades has kept the card ever in the public eye but, in spite of more than 60% of the populations supporting the programme, only a fraction of this number actually carry one. The government's multi-million-pound advertising campaign of 1993 did absolutely nothing to increase the numbers carrying the donor card.

Even though an individual may carry a card and fully desire to help others after his death by offering organs for transplant, their wishes may not be complied with. Doctors faced with the difficult task of breaking the news to the next of kin that their loved one is dead often elect to avoid compounding matters by seeking permission to take organs. Strictly speaking this permission is not required by law but doctors simply will not proceed without it.

Professor Cyril Chantler of Guys Hospital, possibly the leading paediatric renal specialist in the country, explains: "… it doesn't seem to work very well and I am now personally convinced that we should have an opt out system. In other words it should be the convention, it should be the normal practise that after somebody has been pronounced dead their kidneys can be used for others unless they have said they do not wish it to happen."

A Gallup Poll commissioned by the British Kidney Patients Association shows 61% of the population firmly in favour of such a system.

An opt out system already exists in Belgium, Austria, Finland, France, Norway and Singapore. There was an increase of 119% in the number of transplants carried out in Belgium during the first year of the change.

For the kidney patient, dialysis means being connected to a machine for three or more hours up to four times a week and the almost impossibility of leaving a normal life. Professor Chantler is quite clear, "To me the only satisfactory final treatment for somebody with serious kidney disease is a kidney transplant, only kidney transplants will restore normal life."

Over five thousand patients are currently on call for an organ transplant but last year only 2,730 of which 1,765 were kidneys, transplant operations were performed. Many of those still waiting will die before a donor is found. It is true that even with a transplant some of them may still die but without the opportunity of a transplant they are not even given a chance.

Mrs Ward son Timbo died undergoing surgery but call it destiny, call it divine intervention, his life was not without purpose. A devout Christian, his mother, believes he was sent to spur action towards having the donor the card and the formation of a National Association to promote the cause of kidney patience.

Although Mrs Ward now thinks the donor card is moving towards becoming a failure, I feel she is perhaps a little too hard on the development of her own idea. While it may have many failings, from the point of view of the 2,730 patients who did receive a transplant in last year alone it has been a miracle.

But what of the future ? Mrs Ward is now campaigning furiously for the opt out system advocated by Professor Chantler and the government is taking a serious view of the proposals. However, without the full support of the medical profession, in particular the transplant surgeons, a change is not likely for a while yet, perhaps not for another generation.

Until that time it is vital we all give careful consideration at all times to the donor card being carried. Do you have one ? Have you told your relatives about your wishes ?

Sitting at her hospital bedside my daughter turned to me and said; "Look Dad I have a donor card. I've crossed out kidneys, they would not be much use to anyone but they can have everything else !"

It brought a tear to my eye. Having been given back to us by the miracle of a transplant the idea of losing her in some tragic accident is unthinkable. But if it should be, I would have no hesitation at all in seeing her wishes were carried out.

You can pick up a donor card from your doctor's surgery, your local chemist shop or write to either myself or Mrs Ward and we will gladly send you one.

Thirty year update – a BIG update – We ARE The Concrete Cows:

Valley Medical Transport is not around today but when my daughter was called for her kidney transplant it was in that famous Vauxhall car she travelled to hospital.

With Rebekah on call for a donor organ she could not leave the country. I took my two sons to California for a holiday while she remained at home with Mum. Overnight I drove from Yosemite Park to Los Angeles where I tried to catch up on seep laying on Malibu Beach before taking the overnight flight to London Heathrow.

At Terminal Three I was met by a friend who said: "You are not to worry but Rebekah had a kidney transplant last night. There was no way I could have driven to Guys Hospital in London, I was far too knackered. My friend took me home and Valley Medical Transport drove me to London.

Before this transplant I had put myself forward as a live donor. I persuaded ITV News to film a short documentary of the dual operations in support of the work Elizabeth Ward was doing. Unfortunately the surgeons did not go ahead, they were not convinced Rebekah's strong immune system would not reject my organ.

Elizabeth Ward died on 20th July 2020 at the age of ninety-four. She was reunited with her beloved son Timbo. My daughter Rebekah left us in May 2017. I tirelessly promote organ donation but I do not have the strength of Elizabeth Ward so am always finding myself banging my head against a brick wall !

Today in 2024 4,658 patients, of which 98 are children, are waiting for kidney transplants. Over all 7,500 are waiting for organ donations. 4,651 transplant operations were performed. 415 people died while waiting for a donor organ.

CHANNEL FIVE – MILTON KEYNES HOSPITAL RADIO:

There's a degree of one upmanship in this business, explained hospital radio chairman Peter Royal. I know one outfit that works out of a converted kitchen and another that broadcasts from an old linen store, but we can beat them all, our studio is situated in what used to be the gents loo !

Staffed entirely by volunteers and surviving on an annual budget of less than one thousand pounds, Channel 5 Milton Keynes Hospital Radio is looking forward to celebrating its tenth birthday later in the year.

A stay in hospital isn't very much fun for anyone but staff at Milton Keynes General go out of their way to make it as comfortable as possible. An army of volunteers, including the League of Friends, is co-ordinated by a full time member of staff with the second battalion working through the radio station.

Channel 5 broadcasts every evening of the week with a full schedule of programmes at the weekend. Amateur DJs and presenters rushing from work clutching scripts and records but listening to their professionalism on air challenge is difficult to realise they may have spent the last eight hours wrestling within a busy office or factory floor.

I spent a Friday evening eavesdropping on Peter's show, Royals after Nine, listening to a combination of lively chatter, news, music and competitions. Peter and his wife Jenny, who has a spot on Tuesday evenings, have been working in hospital radio for twenty-six years and were founder members of the Milton Keynes station.

They have seen the station grow from programmes on just three evenings a week to its present high profile. But it isn't just playing records that keeps the station alive, volunteers visit the wards informing the patients of the day's programmes and inviting requests. Upon arrival in hospital everyone receives a highly professional programme guide. The next project the management committee is planning is for an outside broadcast unit which will not only be able to cover local events but also take the microphone to the bedsides so involving the patients themselves in the programmes.

Peter Royal explained with the average stay in hospital being less than a week it is important the station is constantly put before patients if broadcasters are not to sit each evening talking to themselves. With the constant flow of requests coming everyday into the Channel 5 office there is little danger of that happening.

The station has composed its own top ten favourites from listeners requests:

Nesun Dorma by Pavarotti
I Just Called To Say I Love You by Stevie Wonder
Lady In Red by Chris de Burgh
Everything I Do by Bryan Adams
Memory by Elaine Paige
Music Of The Night by Michael Crawford
Power Of Love by Jennifer Rush
One Day At A Time by Lena Martell
Bohemian Rhapsody by Queen
The Old Rugged Cross.

While none of his songs appear in the stations top ten, by far the most requested artist is Cliff Richard .

Peter describes his mixture of easy listening and Radio One and a half, somewhere between the BBC's two major music networks.

But Channel 5 is facing something of a problem in broadcasting recently published music. With the changes from vinyl to compact disc the station is having difficulties incorporating the modern and more expensive format into its budget. Although approaches have been made to local record shops none has yet been willing to offer a discount on purchase of CD singles.

With a decade of happy and successful broadcasting behind it Milton Keynes Hospital Radio looks forward to an even brighter future. While his broadcasters hope you will never have to be in hospital and, therefore, listen to them they promise should you find yourself in the wards, there will be happy programmes designed to make your stay a little more present.

FLIE ON THE WALL

I have something of an insatiable interest in the things about me, an inbuilt curiosity. Positively being nosey if you like but it's a quality rather important for a writer. To quench my first I set about writing a series with myself as Fly (Flie) on the wall. All the areas I visited totally fascinated me and I have enjoyed sharing my experience with readers. I have chosen six reports to reproduce here.

In an earlier chapter I discussed how things would have been had Milton Keynes become an airport city with London's third airport sited at Cublington. But aviation is not absent from our area. Looking at its role I wrote two features for the Milton Keynes Citizen discussing the charter airline business and then how pilots are trained to fly heavy jets.

YOUR HOLIDAY STARTS HERE:
As we broke through the cloud cover Table Top Mountain appeared away to my left. Ahead the evening lights of Cape Town twinkled their welcome as the airport runway came into sight. A slight adjustment and we were on our final approach.

Moments later a slight bump and November Bravo was on the ground. The Rolls Royce engines roared as they took up reverse thrust and the giant Boeing 757 came safely to a halt.

Captain Roy King reached across the panel above my head and flicked a number of switches to begin shutting down the aircraft. I just flown halfway around the world without leaving Luton Airport. My flight was in Monarch Airlines eight million pound simulator was so lifelike it was hard to comprehend that I was not on the flight deck of a real aircraft.

The simulator plays an important part in the training of Monarch's two hundred and eighty aircrew. A similar mock-up is used to train cabin crew not only in customer service but also in full emergency procedures.

“Britain is somewhat unique in the past package holiday industry,” explained Danny Bernstein joint managing director of Monarch Airlines, “with the largest share of the market worldwide.”

If you are a regular traveller using the package holiday then the chances are you will have flown with Luton based Monarch Airlines.

Monarch first took to the air in 1968 and today operates twenty aircraft worldwide (with a total market value of 600 million pounds) flying to one hundred destinations, employing two thousand one hundred staff and carrying four and a half million passengers a year.

There is definitely something magical about flying. Perhaps it is the way the modern jet airliner shrinks the world, speeding his passengers thousands of miles in just a few hours. It could be the excitement of visiting far away destinations or perhaps it is the incredulity of suspending hundreds of tons of aircraft several miles above the earth. Perhaps it is the way that airlines, intentionally or otherwise, inject a charismatic charm into every aspect of their operations.

To the travelling public the modern airline is clean, safe and ultra-efficient, very different from the situation that existed twenty-five years ago, with British operators like BA, Virgin Atlantic and Monarch now leading the world.

But in actual fact running an airline is like playing three dimensional chess and takes advantage of skills not evident in other forms of business.

Aircraft have to be in the right places at the right time, meeting airport and air traffic control slots in many different countries and lining up with crews. The crews themselves have to be planned on a rota to meet Civil Aviation Authority regulations and provide a contingency against every eventuality.

Danny Bernstein smiled, “It would be no good trying to explain to three hundred people that their holiday was off because the pilot had to go to the dentist !”

Monarch maintains seven flight and cabin crews for each of its aircraft to give maximum potential flying. The company has achieved the highest utilisation in the world for the Boeing 757 maintaining the balance between profits and competitive fares.

Turning aircraft round from one flight to the next is all important, it is only when such a multi-million pound investment is in the air it is earning money. Something like forty service vehicles have to be brought in alongside the aircraft for this to be done. Each has its specific position and timing on a plan that resembles a military operation. Onboard just seven cleaners can speed through a tired looking cabin making it pristine for his new passengers in less than thirty minutes.

Nine million people take summer package holidays every year and another three million winter breaks. As a charter airline, Monarch serves just about every major tour operator and will fly four and a half million passengers during the course of the year.

That means for the half million people wanting inflight meals and drinks, four and a half million buying duty free goods, four and a half million people with baggage subjected and four and a half million and needing to go to the loo at 35,000 feet !

The high standards achieved by staff at Monarch have made it one of the world's premier charter airlines while others, the likes of Dan Air, Pan Am in the schedule area, who failed to comprehend the importance and have gone out of business.

Even on the shortest of flights there is now inflight entertainment, dietary requirements are planned into any special requests for meals, no take it or leave it here, and every effort is made to make the journey to the destination an important part of the holiday. Getting there can become every bit as exciting as arriving.

While Monarch is our local airline, Luton is not the only UK airport from which the company flies. You will find the familiar black and gold of the company's aircraft at Stansted, Gatwick, Manchester and Newcastle.

All heavy maintenance and administration are based in the area making the company a major local employer. Although none of Monarch's fleet is more than four years old, and some aircraft are now as new as six month old, every aspect has been fully serviced during the winter months in preparation for the summer season.

The commercial planning departments have been hard at work over the past few months coordinating flight paths and slots. Handling agents have been engaged at every airport and crews restrained to the peak of performance. All is now ready for the coming busy holiday season, due to start on 1st May.

Passengers do not actually buy Monarch Airline tickets from their travel agents in the same way as they would British Airways or Virgin Atlantic, flight come as an integral part of the package holiday. You will not see Monarch advertising to the public for business. All staff from the managing director in his office overlooking the runways at Luton, downwards have worked to put the customer first.

When you board your holiday jet you know you will be in safe hands and that your holiday has honestly begun. In the case of Monarch Airlines you will have the hands of over two thousand staff waiting to wave you on your way.

SO YOU WANT TO BE AN AIRLINE PILOT:

When you were younger I wonder if, like me, you had ambitions to become a train driver . Funny isn't it how so many generations of little boys dreamed of driving the six-five special out of London.

Today the ambition of boys and girls in these days age of sexual equality, have moved on to other things.

Among them the glamour of the steam engine foot plate has been exchanged for the flight deck of an intercontinental airliner. Ask an average class of ten year olds who would like to be a pilot and you will be swamped with replies.

But there is something of the mystique about the airline pilot. Where do they come from ? Are they trained or are they born into the job ? After all, keeping hundreds of tons of aircraft in the sky must need some superhuman, if not magical, ability.

The Cab Air group of companies has been training pilots for more than twenty years and in the autumn of 1991 began a school at nearby Cranfield. Cab Air will take somebody with absolutely no flying experience at all and in just over a year turn them out fully qualified to fly commercial aircraft .

At present there are eight young men and women studying at Cranfield to realise their ambitions to fly and the college is constantly on the outlook on the lookout for suitable new recruits.

I am not sure if chief instructor, Captain Dyson, was being honest or just kind when he said I was not too old to learn to fly, but strictly speaking the college is looking for young men and women aged between eighteen and their early thirties, educated to GCSE C grade and above.

The Civil Aviation Authority then requires a class one medical examination before training can commence and of course there are the costs of the fees to be met.

Learning to fly is not cheap and no government grants are available but loans and sponsorship are possible for some.

Once these areas are satisfied you are on your way to the command seat of a Boeing 747 bound for New York, San Francisco, Tokyo or Bombay together with an annual salary in the region of £50,000. For those lucky enough to fly Concorde they can expect to be paid double this figure !

But for the new student at cab air this is a long way off. He will begin flying in one of the school's single engines Grumman Cheetah AA5A. Many hours of flying will be combined with the ground school teaching navigation, aircraft theory, meteorology and instrument rating. Because all civil airlines use only English, foreign students must become fluent not only in general but also technical speech.

The training staff between them have many thousands of flying hours experience on a wide variety of aircraft. As I toured the school I became quickly aware of the calm efficient way the instructors worked with their students installing his sense of self confidence and assurance.

As a student progresses he, or she, moves to the twin engine Grumman Cougar GA7 and learns to fly on commercial airways,. He is taught how to make instrument only landings and to cope with every eventuality in every part of the world.

Progress is continually assessed and recording on a chart in the school's operation room. The school operates a flight simulator which is used to put the student through every eventuality in every part of the world.

Written tests and flight examinations by the Civil Aviation Authority follow before the student graduates as a fully-fledged commercial airline pilot.

The school has a close working relationship with Air UK who every year recruit from the college. But there are Cabair pilots from Cranfield in many of the world's major airlines. Course administrator, Mandy Poole, speaks proudly of one of the college's female students who now flies for British Airways out of London Heathrow.

So you want to be an airline pilot ? Why not give Cab Air a call ? Ring and remember as a commercial airline pilot the sky is the limit

WHAT'S IN A NAME:
It was Emperor Napoleon who declared England to be a nation of shopkeepers, perhaps in the depths of 11 Downing Street the Chancellor of the Exchequer would prefer us to be a nation of shoppers and to spend our way out of recession. But as I look about me I cannot

help but wonder if we have too many shops, too many, that is, for them all to run at a respectable profit.

Although I hate shopping, shops and their history rather fascinate me so I thought I would set off on a trail of investigation to try and find out what lurks behind some of the famous high street names.

In the days when shops used to market goods under their own brand names, Woolworths adopted Winfield from their founder Frank Winfield Woolworth. His policy was to sell goods for just five and ten cents, when translated to outside the Atlantic it became three pence and sixpence. Can you remember which store sold goods under the brand name of Prova ? BHS or, as it was known then, British Home Stores. One of the few stores to retain a brand name is Marks and Spencer with Saint Michael, the Patron Saint of Underwear ? That trading began from a humble market stall.

Another store clinging to its brand name is John Lewis with its Jonelle. Theirs's is a fascinating story taking the name from the founder, John Sneddon Lewis. He was the son of a West Country draper who set up a business in Oxford Street, on his 21st birthday John Lewis senior gave his son a 50% share in the business. When John Spedan Lewis eventually took control of the company he came up with a totally revolutionary idea putting all of his holdings in trust for future employees.

In 1937 the partnership took over the grocery business of Wait, Rose And Taylor which became the popular Waitrose Supermarkets.

Strictly speaking there never was a Miss Selfridge. American Gordon Selfridge founded the Oxford Street department store in the 1920's. The company became part of the Lewis's Department Store Group, later to be taken over by financier Charles Clore. It was Clore, himself, who had the brainchild for chain of high street fashion shops taking the name from the famous London store. Before the first store was opened Clore test marketed his idea with two instore shops in the Birmingham and Liverpool branches of Lewis's. I was present at the midlands launch where all sales girls wore hideous mini-skirted uniforms designed by the millionaire chairman himself. Although smoking was strictly prohibited for everybody else in the store Clore puffed away all evening on a giant Havana cigar .

Richard Branson chose the name Virgin for his business venture because he was a Virgin in the record industry. Remember the early Virgin LP, Tubular Bells by Mike Oldfield ? But don't be misled by the legend, Branson's career was hardly rags to riches. His father was himself a highly successful accountant sending his son to expensive nearby Stowe public school.

Now part of the Midland Banking Group, Thomas Cook began by offering railway excursions. Branching into exotic tours, the name has been a market leader for over a century.

Supermarkets, with their unique idea of self-service, were imported to Britain from the United States in the second half of the 1950's. The first company to trade on this side of the Atlantic operated under the name of Fine Fare.

The Board of Trade definition of a supermarket requires a minimum of two thousand square feet of floor space. The average size of a modern-day Tesco store is in the order of fifty times that size.

The Argos catalogue showroom, whose headquarters are in Milton Keynes, owes the origin of his name to the ancient Greek. Argos means a merchant vessel heavily laden with fine goods. This unique style of shopping is provided proving highly successful.

Did you know that Captain Birdseye's real life ancestor was Clarence Birdseye who invented the world's first commercial food freezer, The Birdseye Patent Plate Froster in 1928. The company founded to market frozen food projects produce still bears his name today.

Lego, the Danish made building toy, has popularised the world over a word derived from ancient Roman language, Latin. Lego means I build.

Never known by its full title MFI stand for More Furniture Ideas.

Gilbert and Sullivan alluded to WH Smith, the founder of the bookselling firm, in their 1878 operetta HMS Pinafore. His progression to First Sea Lord in Disraeli's government had not been unlike that of their comic character Sir Joseph Porter KCB.

We all learned in school history lessons about the Rochdale Pioneers and the founding of the Co-operative movement. The first Co-op came to Milton Keynes in 1883 headed by Thomas Simmonds, a local railway shunter. The caring, sharing Co-op has grown with the New City but took a conscious decision to keep out of the Central Milton Keynes Shopping Centre. Given the inflated rent rises of recent years their wisdom looks have been more than correct.

And what about some of the names are no longer with us? Do you remember Home and Colonial Stores ? Elmo Supermarkets ? Lloyds Corner Houses ? Bejam ? Martins Bank ? John Collier and his famous window to watch ? Peter Lord ?

Shops come and go, some to cease trading, some simply to change their names and marketing strategies while others are swallowed up in takeover bids. So, which high street names common today are destined to evaporate within the next decade ? How will marketing tactics change the way we shop and think ?

Less than twenty years ago England had never heard of McDonald's and burgers were something confined to the unpopularity of school dinners. In 1994 their UK sales will top six hundred million pounds !

So.......

Thirty year update – We ARE The Concrete Cows:
Quite simply how many names from thirty years ago no longer exist in the third decade of the twenty-first

century ? When I wrote Not The Concrete Cows in 1984 people thought that Amazon was a rain forest somewhere or other. So far his year I have placed one hundred and thirty-four separate orders with Amazon !

HOW FAST IS FAST FOOD:

Within the current Thompson Directory for Milton Keynes there are listed no less than twenty-eight fish and chip shops, thirteen Chinese takeaways, three branches of McDonald's, one each of Burger King and Kentucky's Fried Chicken, three Indian takeaways, six pizza shops and ten other assorted outlets offering a variety of food to be eaten off the premises. A staggering sixty-five establishments.

I suppose when anyone mentions fast food the mind instantly turns to McDonald's. There are at present three branches of the burger giant in Milton Keynes including the restaurant thought to be the busiest in the country. Anyone who has tried to get a Big Mac in Central Milton Keynes on a busy Saturday lunchtime could not fail to appreciate this fact and may perhaps, be excused for questioning just how fast is fast food ? The McDonald's Corporation now runs 13,093 in 63 different countries of the world. There are 522 outlets in the United Kingdom alone employing some 1,373 staff.

As well as actually introducing the term fast food to the English language Ronald McDonald (In real life he was Ray Krock who began the business with Dick and Mac McDonald in San Bernardino California in 1954) has added Big Mac and Big Mac Attack to our dictionaries. The marketing department has taught us to say fries instead of chips, to say *to go* instead of *takeaway* and *bun* in place of *bread roll*, with or without sesame seeds !

In a recent survey of 500 households 32% had eaten food from McDonald's in the last week while a staggering 73% tackled burgers and fries within the past month. Only 6% claimed never to have eaten beneath the Golden Arches of McDonald's.

The original business was actually called McDonald's Golden Arches Restaurants but revised to McDonald's Restaurants Limited in 1983. The regional training centre in Sutton Coldfield is still known as Golden Arches House.

Worldwide, two hundred and fifty million customers are served every day and the last audited yearly account showed that they spent $21,885,000,000 ! The Corporation shares are listed on the New York, Frankfurt, Munich Paris and Tokyo stock exchanges but not in London. In 1995, twenty years after the corporation's shares had first been placed on public sale, an initial investment of $2,250 had increased to over $250,000 !

The pizza may have originated in Europe but it took the American touch to turn it into fast food. One particular establishment in San Francisco would deliver your order to your home in a Rolls Royce motor car. So Domino's of Netherfield how about it ? The first drive through (sorry THRU) descended on Milton Kings courtesy of Colonel Sanders and Kentucky Fried

Chicken on Stacey Bushes. Not to be outdone McDonald's followed with two of their own. They have a total of 106 throughout the country. One of my ambitions is to fill a double decker bus with passengers then pull up at the latest restaurant on Rooksley and watch their panic.

Have you ever wondered how the guy behind the counter in the Chinese takeaway takes your order in English scribbled it down in hieroglyphics, bawls through the little hatch to the kitchen staffing in Cantonese and then when the brown paper bag pops back knows which order belongs to who no matter how many customers may be waiting in the shop ? Clever isn't it ? But was the ever popular chinky introduced to us direct from Asia or via Chinatown in a dozen major American cities ?

You may smile at the current TV advert which claims the word burger originates from Germany but it's true ! Fries from the Latin frigo but both needed to make the trip to the USA before entering into common use. Let me make a prophecy, One of the most popular US fast food outlets is Taco Bell selling Mexican dishes at budget prices. Within the next decade Taco Bell will open in Central Milton Keynes. We are already on the way there with The Point offering nachos and hot cheese to go with the big picture so developing the Milton Keynes taste for Mexican spice.

But what of the good old fish and chip shop ? Twenty-eight of them in the city and still the most popular vendor of all takeaway food. The survey showed even higher figures for family eating their food than McDonald's with an amazing 50% having eaten there during the past week. Only one family admitted to never having eaten takeaway fish and chips and its members are strict vegan-vegetarians.

One of the more famous chip shops in Milton Keynes is Pat O'Leary's in West Bletchley. It was regional finalist in the 1992 Fish And Chip Shop Of The Year. After a refit to his premises Mr O'Leary intends entering the contest again in 1994 with hopes of making it through to the national finals. If the attitude of his customers is anything to go by he can have every reason to be competent.

Talking to Mr O'Leary I became aware his belief that the local chip shop is an important part of the community and not just another retail outlet. He sponsors Abbeys School's football team and had received the mayor's award for service to the community.

As well as seeing the invasion of American fast food as competition Mr O'Leary believes it is done much to improve the quality of the traditional fish and chip shop. Gone are the days of the steamy fries and grease laden chips were wrapped in old newspapers. Wherever did the proprietor get all his papers from ? He must have been an avid newspaper reader ! The modern shop is an epitome of hygiene and excellence.

It has been said that what America does today we will copy in ten years time. This is certainly true for the explosion of American fast food throughout Great Britain. But why is that we cannot benefit by exporting our ideas the other way across the Atlantic ? On a visit to California, the birthplace of McDonald's a friend insisted on taking me for lunch to a traditional English fish and chip shop. We drove to the other side of the city only to find it closed !

THE CHIEF:

Since the days of Dixon of Dock Green the TV viewing public has developed a fascination with police drama. From Inspector Morse to Chief Superintendent Adam Dalgleish, from The Bill to Taggart, from Wexford to The Sweeney no other profession quite catches our imagination in the same way. The four series of Anglia Television's The Chief, initially with Tim Pigott Smith and more lately Martin Shaw as Chief Constable Alan Cade has joined in the success and topped the ratings.

But the character and work of our own real-life chief constable Charles Pollard of Thames Valley Police, are very different from his fictional counterpart.

"To be quite honest," Chief Constable Pollard smiled, "Alan Cade is a lousy chief. He is impolite, unpredictable, does not know how to delegate and his meddling makes everyone else look useless in spite of the fact he probably has a high calibre of senior officers about him, if only he would let them get on with it."

After spending an afternoon with Charles Pollard I found myself rather grateful that he was in command of nearly 4,000 officers, 1,500 civilian staff and an annual budget of £196 million that make up Thames Valley Police in 1994. If Alan Cade was in the job I think I would move to live in another area.

So, who is this man who is in charge of law and order and one of the largest police forces in the country ? What kind of man is it who enables us all to sleep safely in our beds at night ?

PC Pollard first pounded the beat in the West End of London out of Bow Street Police Station, the home of the original Bow Street Runners. Every officer, no matter how senior his rank, must always start out as a humble constable but the young Charles Pollard had ambition.

Before sitting his sergeant examinations PC Pollard decided to take a year out and to travel extensively in Central and North America.

Returning to the Metropolitan Police he was selected for a special training course seeking out potential senior officers. As a newly appointed inspector, Charles studied law at Bristol University then served for two years at Paddington.

As a Chief Inspector at New Scotland Yard in charge of public order his was the task of co-ordinating the security at Earl Mountbatten's funeral. A particularly sensitive security task as he had met his death at the hands of IRA terrorists.

Leaving the capital Superintendent Pollard was in command of the Eastbourne Division of Sussex Police before becoming operational support Chief Superintendent and having to deal with the aftermath of the Brighton bombing of the Tory Party conference.

Charles Pollard first came to Thames Valley as Assistant Chief Constable in charge of personnel and training before taking charge of operations. Returning to the Met he took up the post of Deputy Assistant Commissioner in charge of South West London before returning to Thames Valley as Chief Constable.

“The dilemmas facing Alan Cade,” explained Chief Constable Pollard, “are exactly those facing any chief but never in the vast quantity nor the time scales portrayed in the drama. The issues are true to life but not the way they are handled.”

Alan Cade finds it very difficult to establish a home life, flitting from one duty to another. Charles Pollard however puts much of his success down to the tremendous understanding and support of his family. Married with two teenage sons and a seven year old daughter he lives happily in Banbury.

“There have been times in my career,” he commented, “when I have been involved in dealing with major incidents like the Iranian Embassy siege or killing of Blair Peach, when my family hardly saw me for weeks on end. They have been loyal and long suffering.” Perhaps the lack of a happy family life explains Alan Cade’s erratic nature.

Alan Cade found working with female deputy, Anne Stewart, something difficult to cope with. Charles Pollard predicts the time when we will see the nation's first lady chief being only a couple of years away. In another ten years he anticipates several. Milton Keynes, one of the largest areas in Thames Valley Police, is of course commanded by Chief Superintendent Caroline Nicholl. Chief Constable Pollard sees little difficulty had the fictional Mrs Stewart been his deputy .

Charles Pollard regards his career, and that of every offer officer, as a tremendous opportunity to serve the public. “It isn't just arresting criminals,” he explained. “People tend to turn to the police for all kinds of problems and difficulties. When they do it makes you realise that as well as a few rotten apples there are some very fine people out there, the vast majority of the public indeed. I wonder if Alan Cade views things in quite the same way.”

One of Chief Constable Pollard’s predecessors, Peter Imbert who served Thames Valley from late 1980 to 1985, went on to become Commissioner of the Metropolitan Police and received a knighthood for his work. Although PC Pollard's initial ambitions saw him hoping to make it as far as Superintendent, four ranks below that of Chief, one wonders if our own Chief Constable has yet reached the peak of his career.

Thirty year update – We ARE The Concrete Cows:
This was one of three flie on the wall times I spent with our local cops. I went out on a night patrol with two

officers in their car as well as spending an afternoon with Milton Keynes Area Commander. More recently I tried so hard to spend some twenty-first century time with Thames Valley Police but it just never happened.

Watching cop series on TV which is your favourite ? Mine is Foyle's War. Yes, I love Death In Paradise but that's a slightly different genre is it not ?

MAILCOM A MILTON KEYNES SUCCESS STORY:
What's in the post this morning ?

ATM pin number from the bank. Great, now I can use my card to draw cash from the machine.

Mortgage interest rate change no problem providing it's a downward move !

Income tax notification . No comment.

These are just some of the mailings heading out of Malcolm's purpose-built headquarters as I toured their operation in the company of Mark Shotten, the organisations marketing manager.

Also being prepared was a package launching Virgin Atlantic new Hong Kong service. Being a regular flier with Virgin I waited for my own personal mailshot. Sure enough it plopped through my letterbox two days later.

Mark's father was one of the five executive at Marketforce who in early 1982 disagreed with the policies of the company. With little more than the courage in their hands the founding five set up Mailcom in August of that year walking working out of a small factory unit on Mount Farm.

Mark's pride in his company's phenomenal success was hard to disguise. Ten years later complete with six hundred employees and an annual turnover in excess of £12,000,000, Malcolm is the nation's market leader in direct mail service.

With six million items leaving its Winter Hill base every week of the year the company is in the Post Office's top ten users. And with a customer list that looks like who's who in big business, names like Barclaycard, Abbey National and Norwich Union, Mark puts the success of his company firmly down to the success of Milton Keynes. Indeed they share the same philosophy putting people, quality and service for most.

Many of Malcom's original staff of thirty are still with the company seeing their own career succeeding with that of their employers.

If Milton Keynes has been good for Mailcom then certainly Mailcom has been good for Milton Keynes. Not only has it brought consistent employment to the city, even though a period of recession, but its forward looking attitude has brought valuable business to the city.

As one who objects quite strongly to junk mail invading my letter box I was particularly interested to tour Mailcom's business. I cannot go quite so far as to say that I had become a convert to direct mail advertising but now I see there is much more to it than just selling timeshares on the Costa del Whatever.

True enough there were the unsolicited appetising shots, like my Virgin Atlantic package, but these tend to be of a higher professional standard, nothing of the "..you may have won a new car but first you must sit through three hours of hard sell to find your prize is actually a set of glasses valued 99p !

Part of the success of direct mail advertising is down to nothing more than the fact that it works ! Presumably, therefore, the general public likes receiving these sort of mail shots.

Malcolm also deals with what it calls response handling. When you have collected your six cornflake packet tops and sent them off, the chances are it will be Malcolm that posts off your cuddly toy.

"We've dealt with everything here from bonsai trees to folding bicycles," Mark explained

When you dial an 0800 information line to ask about the holiday in Greece or buy the latest CD compilation on your credit card the chances are it will be a Mailcom employee that answers the phone.

But beware Malcolm also operates a credit reference and debt recovery department !
Much of the work requires a high degree of security and confidentiality, nobody would like to think that their bank

statements or credit cards lay about on a work desk to be viewed by anyone. With all sensitive material not only are all employees thoroughly vetted but twenty-four hour security video is in operation.

As my tour of Malcolm came to an end I could not help but feel it is a pity some more employees of other companies about the country did not fall out with their bosses then come to Milton Keynes, as did these founders and show the rest of the world how their business should be run.

Well done Malcolm and thank you for letting Milton Keynes share your success.

TWO WALLS THAT HAVE LOST THEIR FLIES AND ONE OF EMBARASSEMENT:

Not all of my Flie On The Wall features for Milton Keynes Citizen were included in Not The Concrete Cows.

I spent time with a gentleman thatching a local cottage who told me in amazingly great detail how he crafted the roof. So sadly I never included it. The text has been lost or I would have here added it. Sorry Mr Thatcher, that time I spent with you was so special.

Not for the Citizen but something I wrote for the inflight magazine of an American holiday airline. Do airlines have in flight magazines these days ? Flying from London Stanstead to San Francisco I shadowed the flight crew and then on return the cabin team.

Taking off from Stanstead WOW, with the windows on three sides of the cabin the view was so special. Beaten only by coming in over the Pacific Ocean to land at the City By The Bay.

If I am honest the actual piloting of the aircraft was boring, it consisted mainly of adjusting the height and speed to achieve the maximum fuel efficiency. Two pilots and a flight engineer engaged me in lengthy discussions about this, that and the other. A few years ago there had been a disaster where all onboard had been killed when a similar aircraft to ours crashed at sea. The flight engineer got out a manual and showed me in detail what when wrong. Did I really want to know this !

Then flying over the northern ice cap before crossing Northern Canada the pilot said: "If anything were to go wrong I could land on the ice without any problem but we would all be dead from cold long before anyone could get to rescue us. Again did I really want to know this ?

Returning with the cabin crew it was non-stop work. Totally different to the relaxed, casual lifestyle up on the flight deck.

I do so wish I had included these special flies on the Concrete Cows' wall.

AI – Artificial Intelligence - I wish I had never let this within a million miles of our concrete cows ! This is something I penned but it was too long to be published within my Flie-on-the-wall articles. Let me share it with you now then I will tell you of technology's attempt to destroy our Concrete Cows.

This Will Never Catch On – I Wish It Hadn't:
A computer can be said to possess artificial intelligence if it can mimic human responses under specific conditions.

Who said that ? Alan Turing of Bletchley Park.

It was of course the Bletchley Park Mob that gave the world its first computer. Legend says that at the end of the war Prime Minister Winston Churchill ordered the codebreakers computer be destroyed so it did not fall into the hand of enemies. His plan did not work, every second of every day the enemies of Microsoft, Facebook and all the rest make billions ripping us all off.

Let me go back to Leon School for a moment, Leon School during the Cold War. There was a dining room which was never used, there were shutters connecting it to the kitchen which never opened. Everyone used the adjacent dining room. Leon School was originally built to house 1,410 pupils but with the development of our New City and teenagers being bussed in from Tinkers Bridge, Netherfield, Bean Hill, Coffee Hall and Eaglestone that capacity was exceeded. Terrapin temporary classrooms were erected on the playing field so why not turn the unused dining room into a teaching area ? Within the government's civil defence plan this was a place where local people could go in the event of an attack from the Soviet Union to be fed ! I bet there are not many today who know that.

I am speaking now of 1977 when David Bradshaw was Leon's Headmaster. Careful spending meant the school had money left over in its budget. He called a staff meeting to collect ideas as to what it could be spent on.

I was a junior member of staff but I spoke up and suggested, "Perhaps the school could buy a computer."

Bradshaw shot me down in flames. "Don't be so stupid ! If we do that Buckinghamshire County Council will say that if we can waste money in that way our budget for next year needs to be cut !"

With the school student population around fifteen hundred I thought a computer would have been a sound investment. Today Leon School, or Sir Herbert Leon Academy as it likes to call itself, has a student population of but five hundred and thirty-eight, I wonder how many computers it has. I wonder how many of those student have their own mobile phones and I wonder how many know they attend school below which was the location for one of the first signal transmitter and receiver units in Milton Keynes.

The school did eventually buy a computer, they were called PC – Personal Computers, but such was under Headmaster Bruce Abbott as Headmaster, David Bradshaw remained until his retirement firmly anti-computer.

I can so very clearly remember sitting speaking with a young lad who was in my year group, I was Head of Year Nine at the time. He was highly intelligent and I was trying to encourage him to use his abilities to carve a future career for himself.

He said, “One day every home will have its own computer.” Every home, he said and not every person. Politely I explained to him that this was never, ever going to happen.

Harold Wilson gave the world what he called The University On Air, the Open University located in Milton Keynes and one of the first organisations in the New City of Milton Keynes to make wide use of the computer. Today the OU is the largest university by student numbers in the western world. Come now with me for a moment to our city’s university.

Americans may try to claim different but the world knows Britain invented the computer and it happened in Bletchley Park. World famous Bletchley Park, perhaps we should have The City of Bletchley rather than The City of Milton Keynes ! Now that is a thought. Sound's good don't you think ? Right then, let me take my tongue out of my cheek and tell you about something I seriously never thought would catch on.

The other evening I watched the film of the play Educating Rita starring Julie Walters and Michael Caine, Rita was an Open University Student. I am rambling, forgive me, let me get on with the story.

The Open University held a one-day course pulling together different parts of the community in The New

City Of Milton Keynes. I was the education representative. A friend of mine was there on behalf of the police. His name was Alan, we sat together around a square of tables upon each was placed a giant computer monitor. Do you remember when computers used green lettering on a black background ? Such were these state of the art computers we were about to attack.

The professor began speaking, I can remember his words so clearly. *You may have heard of something called The World Wide Web.* Had we ? British scientist Tim Berners-Lee in 1989 (No America you did not invent the internet.) gave us The World Wide Webb. So, I am assuming this all happened sometime in 1990. *Well, the professor continued, I am going to teach you all how to send letters using the world wide web, communications we are calling electronic mail.*

We were all told how to make this extremely difficult and scientifically complex electronic letter system work. We were then told to send an electronic letter to the person sitting next to us, I tried and failed to send an electronic letter to Policeman Alan. Policeman Alan tried and failed to send a message to me. Everyone in the room tried and failed to send an electronic letter to anyone.

I don't see the point, I explained, if I want to speak to someone I telephone them.

But what if they are not by the phone to answer you ?

At work I have a secretary and at home I have an answer machine.

But with electronic mail, *the professor defended,* you can attach a document.

We had not, none of us, managed to send a single message saying *HI* to someone sitting next to us let alone attach a three-volume novel.

Have you never heard of a fax machine ? I said sarcastically. Everyone in the room save the professor agreed with me.

How old are you reading this ? How many of you know what a fax machine is ? (Or was !) If you are under thirty then you were born into a world before the internet and what became e-mail. Jimmy Carter was elected to the White House in 1993 and left office in 2001. I remember him saying that when he became president there was no such thing as a website when he left nobody could live without them. I wonder if there is a fax machine somewhere in The Science Museum.

Have you never heard of a fax machine ? I said sarcastically. Everyone in the room save the professor agreed with me. Trust me, I added, this will never catch on !

Unfortunately it did catch on. Thirty-three years after the invention of the world-wide-web life would be impossible without it. Perhaps that impossibility of life would be better than what we endure today.

The Royal Mail gives us first class post and second class post, both excellent services. That nonsense the professor at the Open University could not get we one-day students to make work is third class mail, no make that thirty-third class mail ! As e-mails come into our lives it is so easy to click and delete them without opening and reading a single word. They have become too routine to be of any importance. True e-mail is convenient and quick but for IMPORTANT matters the traditional letter faithfully processed by Royal Mail will never be replaced. I guess it probably will but I hope never in my lifetime.

That dining room in Leon School, not the unused civil defence area but the busy lunchtime mecca. I wonder if it ever served Spam. Did your school dinners when you were a kid ever serve Spam ?

Spam – S.P.A.M. Specially Prepared American Meat. Something from World War Two it was popular on the dinner plates of the nineteen fifties and sixties. The truth is it was specially prepared rubbish ! OK, so I am a vegetarian these days and would not eat it but even my dog would not go anywhere near Spam.

Spam has come to mean rubbish and every day our electronic mail feasts on Spam.

September 2019 and I was back in Leon School as a Worktree volunteer speaking with a group of sixth form teenagers. As we went around the group introducing ourselves one lad took his smart phone from tapped his fingers on its screen and held it up: "There you go, that's you !" Headmaster David Bradshaw who scorned my idea for a school computer were you looking down on our meeting ?

Yes I use a computer, I am typing these words right now on my Acer laptop. No I do not use a silly-stupid dumbo smart-phone.

Speaking of dumbo silly-stupid smart-phones, the other day I was in my local supermarket when the customer in front of me found his phone battery was dead. He was stuffed and unable to pay for his shopping ! Oh dear what a shame never mind !

When you go shopping do you push the trolley round the supermarket, pick items off the shelves then use the checkout or do you go on-line, click and collect ? Click and collect, shouldn't that be TAP and collect ? Or has technology rewritten the English language to give a new meaning to the word click ?

That local supermarket of mine would fail its GCE English examination. The robot as you reach the payment stage says: *My Morrisons card excepted.* EXCEPTED ! Where's the dictionary ? Hang on.

EXCEPTED – *to not include someone or something*

ACCEPTED - *to take willingly something that is offered; to say yes to an offer, invitation, etc*

It would appear that Spam is not only to be found on this particular supermarket's shelf system but also within the typo brain of its robot !

Electronic mail gave us SPAM. Computers gave us TYPO !

What was it Alan Turing said about artificial intelligence ? The smart phone is the intelligence for the majority of people today, people who its technology has made artificial.

This Will Never Catch On – I Wish It Hadn't !

When I wrote the original book Not The Concrete Cows I typed the words, around forty-five thousand of them, using a typewriter. The pages were then checked and double checked for typos.

Life is a typo – if you do not make any then you are not living it fast enough. True or an excuse for mistakes I leave in my writing ? I do like to leave the odd typo in anything I write for those who take pleasure in finding them.

When it came to Amazon offering Not The Concrete Cows in 2020 Microsoft thought it has invented a new way to type text. No need for a keyboard, I simply sat reading from the original book while my laptop listened and converted the audio into words ready to print. The text then submitted to Amazon was ridiculous, complete and utterly ridiculous ! Artificial Intelligence, artificial it was but intelligent absolutely not never, no way. Microsoft soon abandoned its failing verbal typo infested typing system. Now preparing this updated text to submit to Amazon thirty years after Not The Concrete Cows was originally published I hope I have managed to remove all of Microsoft's errors. If I haven't well remember I do like to leave the odd typo here and there for those who take delight in finding them !

LET'S LOOK AT SOME LEGENDS

Truth is one of the most precious things we own therefore it is only right that we try to be a little economical with it. No that is not a quote from the editor of one of our national tabloids, it comes from a newspaper editor working back in the mid nineteenth century one Samuel Langhorne Clemens better known as Mark Twain.

Mark Twain prefaced his Tudor England adventure The Prince And The Pauper with these words: *I will set down a table it may have happened it might just be a legend but it might have happened.* The wonderful thing about a legend is the truth and fiction become so inextricably entwined it is impossible to tell the difference and so the unedited account becomes a valued part of our heritage. Just where would we be without King Arthur and the Knights of the Round Table ? The likes of the Loch Ness Monster ? Each one looks to go spinning off into future generations for as many as have enjoyed them in years gone by, to continue way into the distant future. Milton Keynes is not without a legend or two of its own. Does a ghost from the Fenny Stratford plague pit honestly haunt the local schools ? Why is an area of Newton Longville known as Dead Queen ? And did Dick Turpin really stay at the Old Swan Inn in Woolston ? Who cares, they are great stories.

Truth is one of the most precious things we own therefore it is only right that we try to be a little economical with it.

RING A RING OF ROSES, A POCKET FULL OF POSIES:

In the late autumn of 1348 a terrible tragedy began to strike down the then sparsely populated area of Milton Keynes. In June of that year a ship docked in Bristol having sailed from France. One of the sailors was sick, he had Bubonic Plague better known as the Black Death. In less than two years that disease spread right across Europe. Two years later one third of this nation's population had been wiped out.

Our Milton Keynes ancestors living in the North Buckinghamshire countryside suffered extensively. It is said that the area about Woburn Sands became established as travellers bypassed plague centres on Watling Street.

A chronicler of the time said the cattle roamed masterless over the countryside, crops rotted in the field for lack of hands to reap them and there were not enough priests alive to bury the dead.

One much acclaimed remedy for the plague involved the use of toads which folk gathered from the local fields. The toad was placed out in the sun to dry then sat upon the bulbous swellings which appeared in the neck, groin and armpits. It was believed that the poison would leave the patient's body and enter the swelling toad.

Another remedy required the application of a concoction made from figs, yeast, onions and butter.

A third and grossly more painful remedy saw the whipping of the victim's naked body. It was thought that as the plague was a judgement from God substituting the physical pain of flagellation and begging divine forgiveness could offer a hope of a cure. Little doubt our ancestors tried all of these and others but without success. The numbers of the dead were so vast that bodies were communally buried in deep pits. Legend dictates that the Fenny Stratford pit was located in a field slightly to the west of the town.

More than five hundred years later in 1897, the Fenny Stratford School Board put up a school on that land and then the trouble started.

Very soon Victorian teachers and their children became aware of an unearthly presence in their midst. Doors would creak open then strangely bang closed again. Fleeting glimpses could be snatched from time to time of a small female figure chasing after the children as they went out to play.

Somebody decided to name the ghostly apparition Mary and explained her appearance is a child who had died during the Black Death then had been buried in the Fenny Stratford pit. It was claimed that she was lonely, not being able to play anymore with her friends and so she sought new companions among the children of the school.

Mary was the only child of a blacksmith who lived by the side of the lane that ran from Fenny Stratford to the village of Bletchley. She was a happy child although lonely not having any brothers or sisters. She was a popular figure in the area, her father had been a respected member of the community.

Mary's mother was the first member of the family to be struck down by the plague. Two weeks later both she and her husband were dead leaving Mary an orphan. Mary wandered about in a state of helplessness grief before she too fell to the terrible disease.

Over the years since 1887 the Fenny Stratford school underwent several changes but Mary steadfastly remained as an extra pupil. When the school moved to new buildings on Bletchley's Lakes Estate it is claimed that Mary went with it to the site of Leon School in Fern Grove. Nobody has actually seen Mary for several years but doors sill inextricably open and footsteps are heard running down the deserted corridors as this particular lonely ghost chases after her friends.

Well there we are, I have set down my tale you can believe it or not if you wish. It may have happened, it might just be a legend but it could have happened ! Let me now move on and tell you about a very different lady.

IN SEARCH OF A DEAD QUEEN:

We all know Queen Boudica from school history lessons. That fearsome lady with knives on the wheels of her chariot, that famous warrior championing the plight of the Ancient Britons against the mighty empire of Rome. The widow who suffered under the whip and saw her daughters abused, who now is immortalised in the bronze statue adjacent to Hyde Park Corner.

But what you may ask has Boudica got to do with Milton Keynes ? Where does her legend touch our area ? Draw a little closer and I will tell you.

Nero was the Roman emperor (presumably sometime before he took up violin lessons) and a certain Suetonuis Pauligus (Where did they get names like that from ?) was the governor of Britain. This was in about AD 60. Prastigus (Like I said where did they get those sort of names from ?) was the King of the Iceni Tribe of East Anglia and his wife was the famous Boudica.

A Roman writer described the Iceni Queen as a tall woman with piercing eyes and a loud voice. A great massive mop of red hair hung down to below her waist. Round her neck was a large gold torc. (A torc is a stiff metal ring.) She wore a full flowing tartan dress and over it a thick cloak fastened with a brooch.

When King Prastigus died he expediently left half of his property to Nero and willed that the reminder should be divided between his two daughters.

This appeared to have been more than generous, perhaps intended to ensure the future wellbeing under the Roman occupation of his family. However, half was not enough for the governor who took the lot !

When Boudica and her over-taxed tribesmen made protest the Icini Queen was whipped and her two daughters raped by Roman officers. Boudica's resulting rebellion very nearly evicted the Roman Empire from the shores of Britain.

Boudica and her followers marched on the Roman capital of Colchester which they sacked and burned. The 9th Legion sent to put down the uprising was all but wiped out by the Britons as they marched towards London. Governor Paulinus, who was at that time in Mona (The capital of Anglesey), ordered a strong cavalry troop to accompany him to London. They found the city in a state of dire panic.

Marching his southern troops along Watling Street Paulinus intended to meet up with the army now moving post-haste towards Boudica. It was his intention for the larger army to engage with her stronger force. In so doing London was left to its fate and was burned along with Saint Albans, the Roman fortress in Verulamium. If the Roman historian Tacticus is correct no less than seventy thousand Roman Citizens had so far perished under the anger of Boudica.

Surging through Milton Keynes Boudica met up with Paulinus and his army near to Towcester. Never before in the history of Roman Empire had such humiliation been suffered and if Governor Paulinus could not turn events it will be better he perish in the fray than have to report back to Nero.

Boudica outnumbered Paulinus ten to one but hers were undisciplined tribal farmers and herdsmen against the might of two highly trained Roman legions. She addressed the troops: *We British are used to women commanders in war. I am not fighting as an ordinary person for my lost freedom, my bruised body and my outraged daughters. The gods will grant us the revenge we deserve. Think how many of you there are and why we are fighting; then you will be able to win this battle, or die. That is what I, a woman, plan to do. Let men live in slavery if they want to.*

But the pride of every Roman soldier was hurt and that of Governor Paulinus above them all. There would be no prisoners, there would be no slaves. If Roman rule was to survive the rebellion had to be crushed entirely and without mercy. The account of Tacticus records that eighty thousand Britons are slain with just four hundred Romans but perhaps it would be only right to credit him with just a little creative accounting.

Boudica was not among those lost in battle. After outfighting any man she escaped and made her way across country south to Newton Longville where she poisoned herself. At least that is what the official story put out by the Romans said, perhaps to discredit their enemy by branding her a coward. Another writer Dio Cassius, telling the tale a century and a half later, explained that Boudica died from a sickness several weeks after the battle, perhaps as a result of wounds turning septic. She was then secretly buried in Newton Longville and greatly mourned.

Governor Paulinus did not stop there. He slaughtered thousands upon thousands more Britons in revenge before reporting back to Nero that this particular part of the empire was again at peace.

STAND AND DELIVER:

The publishers of my children's novels have their editorial artistic and design offices in the North of England, when I have meetings there I tend to leave home in the small hours in the morning in order to make a prompt nine o'clock start. I was the only car on a lonely road just outside York when in the faint glow of the coming dawn I swerved to miss a horse and rider. Cursing the road sense of this particular rider, I looked back into my mirror and watched both figures, rider and horse, disappear into the darkness.

Had it really been a member of the pony club out for an early morning trot or had I just encountered the ghost of one of the many highway men who ply their trade up and down the roads of England ? With the spirit of Mark Twain that truth is such a precious commodity we should be economical in its use, I reached for my dictaphone to record the experience.

The wind was a torrent of darkness among the gusty trees. The moon was a ghostly galleon tossed upon cloudy seas. The road was a ribbon of moonlight across a lonely moor. As the highwayman came riding, riding up to the old indoor. So wrote Alfred Noyes in his famous poem. I wonder if he was inspired by a similar experience to my own.

Returning to Milton Keynes I shared my thoughts but far from being shipped off to the funny farm I found I had something in common with many others. A former landlady of the Shoulder Of Mutton public house in Little Horwood explained it was quite common for people to come into the bar saying they had hit a phantom rider with their car. That was before they had a drink !

Pony trekkers to the south of the area have claimed another apparition gallops the Quantock Hills. This apparently is Catherine Furnace the Hertfordshire highway woman who was shot and killed during the hold up in 1659 when she was twenty-five years old. It is thought that her ghost is in search of that of Dick Turpin.

Since the days when the Romans first laid down Watling Street, Milton Keynes has been a major point upon the country's main arterial routes. But the road hardly resembles the A5 trunk road we know today.

An Act of Parliament in 1706 set up the Hockliffe to Two Mile Ash Turnpike but it was an unmetalled road riddled with deep potholes and puddles. In the immediate years after 1800 the inhabitants of Little Brickhill, Great Brickhill, Soulbury, Bletchley, Simpson, Loughton, Shenley, Bradwell and Calverton were all indicted at the Quarter Sessions for not repairing the highway. But the road was perfect for the trade of the highwayman, the most notorious of who was the legendary Dick Turpin.

Dick Turpin robbed stagecoaches along the entire route from London to York. Was it he that I had met on my early morning drive ? Is it the ghost of this particular masked robber that haunts the roads about Little Horwood ?

Legend described him as a suave well-spoken gentleman relieving travellers, in the nicest possible way, of their belongings. In truth he was probably an unshaven and dirty wretch of small stature and pathetic countenance.

But whatever his appearance he was certainly only too well known to the local innkeepers. From Fenny Stratford to Stony Stratford and from Little Brickhill to Calverton he had his safe houses. One of these it is claimed is the Old Swan at Woughton On The Green.

Highway robbery was of course a capital offence and the site of the gallows at Denby Hall, near Bletchley on the Hockliffe to Two Mile Ash Turnpike was a constant reminder to our Mr Turpin of the fate awaiting him at the end of his career.

It was a bright moonlit night and the redcoats were out with a warrant from Little Linford magistrates Justice of the Peace Knapps. Their quarry was the accursed Richard Turpin on whose head was a bounty of five hundred guineas. To stay on the main Turnpike would mean certain capture and so he headed north across country to Woughton.

With a flurry of his coat, Dick Turpin astride his trusty mare Black Bess clattered into the cobbled yard at the rear of The Old Swan. Quickly dismounting, he led the horse into the stables where, assisted by the innkeeper, he nailed four new horseshoes on top of Bess's existing shoes. But he nailed them on in reverse. After a quart of the landlord's best ale Dick galloped off towards

Willen leaving a false trail and throwing the redcoats into confusion.

It is a wonderful little story and one that has been told in Milton Keynes for the past two centuries. However, the same tale is told about a dozen similar inns up and down the entire length of the road from London to York. The present-day landlord Geoff Bevan is something of a local expert on the legendary Richard Turpin. When he took over Ye Olde Swan he set off in search of the infamous highway men and the stories surrounding the inn. Although researchers from BBC television series Living Legends have been unable to find it, Geoff located Turpin's grave in the old Saint George's Church are near the city wall in York. Mysteriously someone places fresh flowers on the grave every month.

Geoff pointed out a large stone near the front of the pub. *That.* he explained. *is the old mounting block from which Turpin would climb astride Black Bess.* He went on to recount how the stone is supposedly haunted.

Anyone who moves it does so at their own peril. when the council came to tarmac the road they worked around it fearing they would disturb the curse.

Dick Turpin was finally arrested for stealing a mare and foal, brought before York Assizes and hanged on the 7th April 1739. He was taken from York Castle to the gallows in a cart from which he waved to the onlookers, doffing his hat and bowing. Once on the scaffold he calmly launched into a thirty minute conversation with hangman Matthew Blackburn before jumping off himself to his death. His letters weighing some twenty-eight pounds can still be seen in York Museum. Reports at the time claimed that his body was dug up and taken to a surgeon for dissection only to be seized again and re-buried in quick lime.

The tale of our friend Mr Turpin makes a lovely little story and the difficulty of disentangling fact from fiction is near impossible. Does it matter in the slightest ? Such is the magic and the power of the legend. Why not drop into Ye Old Swan dating back to the 14th century and one of the oldest buildings in the City of Milton Keynes ? Go and share a tale or two with Jack Bevan about the inn's most famous patron.

Oh and by the way I wonder just how many of you have effigies of Dick Turpin and his illustrious colleagues sitting up on your mantle shelves ! To be the toby was 18th century criminal slang for highway robbery. From it today we get Toby Jugs.

IN SEARCH OF THE SUPERNATURAL:

I was on the lookout in some fields across the river and not far from Milton Keynes. At last I came across some holes on the other side of the hedge by the side of the road and they looked like places for rabbits. So me, my brother and Billy Blunt made an arrangement to go there next Sunday.

We took ferrets in a bag and two dogs. Setting out about at about ten o'clock Milton Keynes Church bells were ringing for the main service. As we didn't want to be seen we climbed over the gate and looked about us but nobody was in sight. I took the ferret out the bag. I knelt down at one of the holes put the ferret in then looked up to see a big man, like a great big blacksmith, standing a few yards from our backs.

We were fairly caught and expected him to ask our names for we thought he was on the lookout for poachers. We went to get the ferret back and in so doing took our eyes off him but in just a moment and when we looked up he was nowhere to be seen. We ran to the gate to see if he were in the road but he had completely vanished. Old Billy was frit to death and so was my brother and I can tell you I was dead scared.

This is an unearthly encounter reported to have taken place near to Milton Keynes Village more than one hundred years ago and for certain this trio never poached again in that field ! The tale was told in the local pubs and written down during the 1920's in a little book Sketches of the Buckinghamshire Countryside.

Another story is to be told of a ghost Ole Curley who would roam the Newport Road about Woolstone in the company of a small dog. Part of the hedgerow was for many years known as Curly Bush. Curly was said to favour dark, moonless nights. Although the last time he was definitely seen was in 1850 there was a close encounter in 1919.
The story claims that a veteran of the Great War had been from his home in Woughton to Fenny Stratford in order to collect his army pension. On his return he apparently spent most of it in the bar at the Swan. Attempting a shortcut through the churchyard he slipped, fell into a bush and slumbered into a drunken stupor. More than one person thought they had found Ole Curly !

It would seem that Woughton and Woolstone have more than their fair share of spirit visitations, several people claimed to have seen a hooded horsemen ride across Newport Road in the direction of Milton Keynes Village. The crossroads there had been the site in the 16th century of a gibbet where many a poor fellow was dispatched from mortal existence.

Among these would have been the victims of Henry Turpyn, priest of Woughton Church, the local witchfinder general and seeker out of evil. (Not to be confused with Dick Turpin.)

The landlord of one of the older inns in Milton Keynes went down to his bar one morning to find all the stools on the floor about the tables yet knowing they had been put on top of the tables when he locked up the previous evening.

The next night he awoke and thought he heard the television set playing. However, a closer listening revealed the sounds of a party going on in the bar and the clanking of pewter mugs on the bar tables. He declined to investigate any further !

But the area's ghosts are not confined to Woughton. Drivers on a lane between Buckingham Road and Little Horwood will be familiar with the slight dip in the road, a dip the Highways Department has tried several times to remove.

The story goes that there was a beautiful girl from Horwood who fell deeply in love with a young man below her social standing. Forbidden by her parents to marry, the young couple eloped one night but were chased by the angry father. In the chase the bride's coach overturned and that on the young girl a mortally wounded. With her dying breath she cursed the spot declaring the road would never again have a smooth surface.

Fanny Leon came to Bletchley with her husband, Herbert, in 1882. For more than fifty years she made her home in Bletchley Park. She served as a JP, school governor and there was not a single aspect of the town's business in which she did not concern herself. When she died in January 1937 Bletchley lost a dear friend and her estate was put up for sale.

Eventually the property was taken over by the secret services housing the enigma German wartime decoding machine. Now in the care of the Bletchley Park Trust, the house was for many years the regional training centre for British Telecom. Staff had repeated several sightings of an Edwardian lady in full evening dress descending the oak staircase. They are perfectly certain it is Fanny Lady Leon.

I asked someone who, as a young man, had known the Leon Family when the members lived at Bletchley Park if he thought that Lady Leon would have wanted to haunt her old home. *Put it this way* he smiled *if the old girl could find anyway to stay on a check up on all is happening she would do it* .

If you believe in ghosts then are these the only members of the spirit world to reside in Milton Keynes ?

In the summer of 1988 construction work at Wavendon Gate was temporarily suspended when builders uncovered Roman burial remains. Do these members of Caesar's far flung empire still linger about the area ? And what of the Bronze Age burial mounds in Old Wolverton, Cotton Valley and Milton Keynes Village ? Or the skeleton a young lady found at Blue Bridge ? Or the Saxon woman uncovered at Tickford near Newport Pagnell ? And what of the entire Saxon family excavated in 1990 at Shenley ?

Is there any trace of their wanderings abroad now their rest has been disturbed after so many centuries? Or are such apparition nothing more than the illusions of an overactive imagination ? What do you think ? Are you sure ?

MEMORIES OF WARTIME MILTON KEYNES

Thirty year author's note – We ARE The Concrete Cows:
I am part of the last generation who can remember the last generation who could remember the Great War – World War One. Thirty years ago I was so privileged to be able to spend time with those who could remember Wartime Milton Keynes, or should I say the area of North Buckinghamshire which in January 1967 Harold Wilson's government would designate for the building of the New City of Milton Keynes.

Speaking with one couple the lady interrupted her husband telling him that he was getting the two wars mixed up. Senior moment ? Perhaps. Can you imagine what it must have been like to have lived through two world wars ?

Now for the introduction to this section I wrote thirty years ago for Not The Concrete Cows.

MEMORIES OF WARTIME MILTON KEYNES

During the research I originally undertook at the time I was writing an autobiography of the Leon family of Bletchley Park I was privileged to be introduced to many wonderful people who shared with me their memories and stories of how our city area was in bygone years.

One of these was Miss E M Wing of Eaton Avenue, Bletchley. For many years Miss Wing taught in the Bletchley Road School, now Knowles and at one time Leon, before becoming the first deputy head of Water Eaton, later to be known as Eaton Mill Combined School.

Miss Wing is a tremendous character with a memory stacked with fascinating tales of education in Bletchley during the war years of 1939 to 1945. With her kind permission, and using the school record books of the time, I began to chronicle parts of those awesome years.

BOMBING:
Air bombardment by the German Luftwaffe of our cities was an immediate threat at the outbreak of war. Newsreels had shown how Hitler's Air Force had stormed across Europe so Great Britain steeled herself

to repel any similar attempt to overrun our island home. ARP wardens were recruited, Anderson shelters were delivered and sirens tested. Buckinghamshire County Council issued its schools with specific instructions both for precautions and what to do in the event of an actual raid .

Sirens sounded in anger for the first time only moments after the actual declaration of war was announced. One of the Bletchley sirens was located on the roof of the council offices, now the Masonic Hall, at the Fenny Stratford end of Bletchley Road (Queensway). For the children in the nearby school the noise of the wailing was deafening.

Staff took time off from teaching the three R's to sit the children down with sheets of brown paper, scissors and pots of glue. With care they cut thin strips and pasted them to the glass on every window in the school as a precaution again bomb blast.

Bletchley being at that time a rural town, did not expect to be a priority on the Nazi hit list and so special air raid shelters were not issued to the schools. The headmaster at Bletchley Road School, Ernest Cook, took advice and designated the main school corridor as the strongest and safest place in the building. When the siren sounded teachers would gather up their charges and sit them in lines on the floor down the length of this makeshift shelter.

An early warning was recorded in the school log as: *The air raid siren went off at 10:50am, the children were immediately taken to their positions and were assembled in an orderly manner within two minutes. The all clear siren went at 11:27am. During the air raid community singing was thoroughly enjoyed, the children entering lustily into the whole atmosphere. There was no sign of panic, in fact I was delighted with the whole demeanour of the children.*

Although on this particular day everything appeared to go off without incident later a strange combination of fear mixed with excitement during alerts made a continuance of any teaching or organised activity near impossible. Eventually lessons were abandoned and boxes of comics placed at intervals along the floor to be read during raid alerts.

Picture then the situation: In the middle of an algebra test the warning siren sounds, it's piercing wine deafening all in the school from its location just twenty-five yards across the road. Books are hastily packed away, desk lids closed, excited children organised and comics distributed. Secure in the knowledge that Bletchley was unlikely to be bombed, pupils went happily to school hoping that the alarm would go off and give them the chance to catch up on the adventures of Desperate Dan or Roy of the Rovers.

The headmaster carefully recorded every warning in the school logbook:

October the 14th 1940 Air Raid Warning 10:50 AM All Clear 11:10 AM Air Raid Warning 11:20 AM All Clear 11:30 PM Air Raid Warning 12:35 PM All Clear 2:05 PM

November the 6th 1940 Air Raid Warning 11:10 AM All Clear 11:25 AM Air Raid Warning 2:20 PM All Clear 3:25 PM

January the 21st 1941 Air Raid Warning 10.23 AM All Clear 10:47 AM Air Raid Warning 11:37 AM All Clear 12:20 PM Air Raid Warning 1:43 PM All Clear 2:08 PM Air Raid Warning 3:35 PM All Clear 4:15 PM

On one particular day there were so many warnings that he gave up any hope of teaching, closed the school and sent all the children home. Perhaps the Germans were not so bad after all !

But while Bletchley was essentially at the centre of the farming community, and there was little strategic advantage in attacking fields of wheat or grazing cattle, had the German Intelligence learned of what was going on at Bletchley Park the town would have been blasted off the face of the earth ! Winston Churchill referred to this work as his most ultra-secret. Hundreds of cryptologists were beavering away cracking the codes of intercepted enemy communications.

Ignorant of the significance of Bletchley, the German bombers simply passed overhead on their way to the industrial targets of the Midlands or nearby RAF bases. These flights set off the air raid warnings without any real danger of attack. But there was one occasion when a lone German aircraft did attempt to bomb the town. Miss Wing retells the story as if it had happened but only yesterday.

It was a cold crisp morning, one of those cloudless days when the winter sky is clear and bright blue. Muffled against the frost the children of Bletchley Road School were out playing in the yard. One by one they left their games to listen as the sound of an approaching aircraft filled the air, eventually someone spotted it coming in low over the horizon. A single Heinkel, markings clearly visible, bomb doors open and its lethal cargo still in place. It must have become detached from its group and was looking for a suitable target before returning home to the Fatherland. The navigator and bomb aimer conferred, perhaps fuel was running low, they then decided to hit Bletchley.

The pilot brought the plane in for its initial bomb run but seeing children playing in the school yard, quickly put the aircraft into a steep turn and veered away. Enemy or not, Nazis did not intentionally kill innocent children. The bombs were dropped on a cabbage field near to Skew Bridge on the Drayton Road before the plane returned to Germany.

I've spoken to others who told me the plane was aiming for the railway line, thinking it a better target than the town, but that doesn't make such a nice story does it ?

The teachers and children of Bletchley Road School threw themselves wholeheartedly into the war effort. They were adopted by Royal Navy battleship SS Chelwood and also held a number of fundraising activities to buy items and equipment for the RAF.

Recorded in the school logbook: *This morning at 9:30 AM a very pleasing ceremony took place. The presentation of a rubber dinghy to the RAF by the school. The idea was conceived by a boy named Horn in form 1A. It was announced to the school that during the Christmas Holidays a competition would be arranged, the making of toys of all kinds out of scrap metal. When these had all been brought into the school an exhibition followed by a sale of work would be held. Prize winners would be awarded saving stamps this was duly held and £30 pounds raised.*

The ceremony was held at morning assembly when Squadron Leader Benyon and Squadron Leader Moore were present to receive the gift on behalf of the RAF.

In the afternoon Squadron Leader Benyon lectured to the children on the use of the rubber dinghy. A demonstration vessel was floated on the static water tank and representatives from each class allowed inside. Miss Mora Hirling from General de Gaulle's headquarters also attended and lectured on the Free French.

A year later representative of the RAF was back in school again to benefit from the children's generosity.

The headmaster wrote in the school's log book: *March 29th 1944 at 3:15 PM this afternoon a cheque for thirty-six pounds and fifteen shillings was prevented to Wing Commander C C Howes for the RAF to purchase a parachute.*

EVACUEES:

In common with many others up and down the country the Bletchley Road School was closed on 4th

September 1939 as part of the war emergency, it reopened on 22nd September with the following recorded by the headmaster , Ernest Cook, in the official log book.

September 22nd 1939 school reopened owing to the presence of two official evacuated schools from London. The Bletchley Senior School is meeting only from 9:00 AM to 12:30 PM.

27th September 1939 Mr J Haynes Assistant Secretary for Education visited the school. A conference was held between the heads of the Bletchley Schools and the evacuated London School to discuss the many problems arising from working in double sessions.

With the area not expecting to be up front of bombing, Bletchley was one of the billets selected for housing some of the countless children evacuated from the nation's capital. Local schools strained to cope with the extra pupils. The deacons of Spurgeon Memorial Baptist Church in Aylesbury Street came quickly to help, offering their rooms to the school and lessons commenced there on 2nd November. School inspectors from London toured with the Bletchley Headmaster on November 21st all other church halls in the district pressing them into service. Among those initially secured were Temperance Hall in George Street and the cricket pavilion in Bletchley Park. All this at a time when many of the young men teachers were going off to join the service and leaving the school terribly short of staff or staff. It was late one evening when the first special evacuee train pulled into Bletchley Station. In crocodile fashion the children marched to Bletchley

Market in Oliver Road (The site of the present-day Sainsbury's Supermarket) where they were met and organised for the night. Being so late it was not possible to find homes for all of the children until the next day and so it was decided they should spend the night in the school.

In the charge of a small handful of lady teachers the assortment of children settled into makeshift beds within Bletchley Road School. With a definite sense of what was right and proper lady teachers were set about insisting each child wash his, or her, hands and face before bed. Unfortunately, there were only a very few wash basins and no hot water. Using the organisational skills inbred into every school teacher a rota was drawn up.

"Excuse me but you wash me next lady."

The child addressed one of the young lady teachers, Miss Wing, who looked down at this pathetic little face. Turning over the brown parcel label attached to the young boy's coat lapel she read his date of birth. Goodness this child was only four years old, his birthday had been the day before and he had been evacuated from London entirely on his own without any parent, brother or sister ! What a terrible mistake. But the mistake was there and asking for his face to be washed before bedtime.

Although she had forced herself to adopt a hard exterior in order to cope with the emergency of dozens of pitiful children away from home in a strange place and not knowing when, if ever, they would see their parents again Miss Wing was moved close to tears. She took the little boy, we will call him Harry, home with her the next morning where he lived with her family for the rest of the war. From then on, she became his adoptive mother and they are still in close contact today more than half a century later.

David Prophet, of Highbury London, was a *vaccy* in Bletchley from September 1939 to January 1943. He remembers very clearly leaving London on Friday 1st September 1939 bound for somewhere in England. That somewhere turned out to be Bletchley. For his time in Milton Keynes he lived at 36 Windsor Street with a couple, Hilda and Eric Aldreman. He has the fondest memories of his stay and still makes regular visits to the area.

Fred and Sylvia Warren of Stoke Goldington took in several evacuee children and are still in contact with many of them, one of whom now lives in Perth Australia.

The worsening international situation during the spring of 1940 saw a degree of chaos descend upon what was a highly organised school. As the German forces swept across France, government instructions went out that schools within the evacuation areas were not too close for the Whitsuntide Holidays. Unfortunately, two of the Bletchley Road teachers had already left to visit families in other parts of the country. Conflicting instructions were issued over the BBC and while the school remained open only 50% of children attended.

The school cancelled its sports day scheduled for 31st May in fear for the worsening situation at Dunkirk. It must have been a terrible time as Britain prepared, after the fall of France, to stand alone.

On 12th June the Education Committee ordered the school be officially closed until further notice to facilitate additional preparations to receive more evacuees. But all the teachers continued to work with children attending on a voluntary basis. No less than 94% attendance is recorded for that week but very few classes were held. Instead to support of the government's dig for victory campaign every spare space within the school grounds was dug up and prepared for cultivation.

The headmaster recorded on the 17th June 1940: *Received circular letter 483/1940 this states that children should be encouraged to attend school as usual but the registers would not be marked. The response from the children was very good. The normal timetable was worked as far as possible with exception that extra time was devoted to the gardens.*

Four days later normal schooling was resumed as the nation stood ready for the Battle of Britain.

But it wasn't only children who came to live in Milton Keynes. With this being a farming area there was an invasion of land army girls, there was an RAF group signals camp in the area now occupied by Lord Grey and Rickley Schools while Bletchley Park became a major centre of counter intelligence. Among those working at Bletchley Park and billeted in Milton Keynes

was Roy Jenkins, later to become Labour MP, Home Secretary and founder member of the SDP. He is now chancellor of Oxford University.
There was scarcely a spare bed in the area ! On the 29th August 1940 the Ministry of Health sent a psychoanalyst to Bletchley to check on the condition of the evacuees. Her report must have been satisfactory because the school log reports more evacuee children arriving on October 7th, 8th, 9th and 10th, bringing the total attending the school to eighty. By the end of the year the number had crept up to nearly one hundred, representing 25% of the school role. A similar situation existed in every other school throughout the area.

But within the year the number of evacuees had dropped to just nine children then to eight and to seven. By the end of the 1943 summer term it was down to four and two by Christmas. Even these are departed by the next summer holiday.

Victory in Europe was announced on 8th May1945. Bletchley Road School was closed for two days to mark the end of the war with Germany. The following week the school held its own special celebrations.

The headmaster wrote in the school log: *This afternoon in place of the usual timetable a special victory celebration was held. It took the form of a general sports day, mass country dancing and picnic tea.*

Just about every street erected trestle tables along the footpath, laden with as much food as rationing would permit and a rare good time was had by all. The local paper reported dancing in Brooklyn's Road, games in

Clifford Avenue, a bonfire in Water Eaton Road and a bun feast in Duncombe Street. Each party raised money for a special fund to welcome back the menfolk of the town on their return from the forces.

Another fund was started when a reader walked into the Bletchley Gazette newspaper offices and gave five pounds towards a party for the evacuees. Others added to this enabling all to be brought back for super party in Saint Martin's Hall. Every child was given an inscribed book as a keepsake and memento of their time in Buckinghamshire.
So the children of Milton Keynes settled down to peacetime and those who spent part of the war years in our locality, as evacuees, returned to their homes. The marathon organisation behind accommodating the extra children concluded.

As soon as war with Germany became inevitable the authorities set down contingency plans for the safety of its children. The Lord Privy Seal's Office issued Public Information Leaflet number three, *Evacuation why and how ?* In July 1939. words had been chosen with some considerable care to persuade parents of the merit in moving children out of the areas likely to suffer bombing and into places of relative safety.

Officials had previously toured the area of Milton Keynes canvassing households as to available space for evacuees. The information leaflet explained: *There is room in the safer areas for children: householders have volunteered to provide it. They have offered homes where the children will be made welcome. The children will have their school teachers and other helpers with them and their schooling will be continued.*

Daphne Capp, whose father kept Home Farm in Newton Longville, remembers well the day the evacuees descended on their village. The householders had been expecting children but when the bus turned up with mothers and babies, one by one the villagers drifted away without their offering a billet. It took the Newton reception committee well into the late evening before the last visitor was accommodated.

FIRE WATCH:
Now that the events of World War II have passed into history it is almost laughable how inadequate the nation's preparations for war actually were. We derive a lot of innocent amusement from the antics of Dad's Army but just how near are they to the truth ?

Buckinghamshire County Council issued a memo from its Education Department on the 26th June 1939 to all its teachers outlining certain contingency measures in the event of war. A week later six members of the staff of Bletchley Road School, Mr E C Cook, Mr E C Jones, Mr B G Davis, Mr A Jones, Miss Evans and Mr White enrolled for training as ARP wardens.

Every school was required to have at least one of its teachers trained as an ARP warden so Bletchley fared extraordinarily well. Training classes for our area were held at Wolverton County Girls School on three Saturday mornings in July. A grand total of six hours training was all that was deemed necessary to cope with the coming emergency.

Teachers were invited to train in additional first aid and first aid kits were issued to every school. Also each school was ordered to receive one copy of the Saint Johns First Aid Handbook !

In Slough, which at the time was part of Buckinghamshire, trenches were dug at every school in which the children would shelter during air raids. Primitive though this was it was not considered necessary to go to the expense of having similar trenches dug in North Buckinghamshire !

Paragraph four of this memo declared: *Arrangements are being made by the Education Committee to supply sprinkler pumps and buckets to schools in the county which are in the more thickly populated areas.*

Although Bletchley in the summer of 1939 could not by any stretch of the imagination, be regarded as thickly populated the Bletchley Road School did indeed receive their pumps and buckets.

The headmaster thought receipt worthy of mention in the school logbook, he wrote: *October 18th 1939 twelve buckets of various sizes were delivered from Aylesbury today.*

Although the local authorities did not seriously expect any heavy bombing, they did appear to be very worried about firebombing. Each area had firewatchers whose duty it was to be on the lookout for fires and put them out before any serious damage could take hold. But as more of the menfolk joined the forces the numbers left for civil defence duties were limited. On 13th August 1942 the Bletchley Fire Prevention Officer met with Ernest Cook, Headmaster, ARP Warden and Evacuee Billeting Officer, to discuss the future of fire watching in the south of our area. Another minute exists of a second meeting on the 9th October 1942 when they decided that women could be engaged.

After calling off his plans for an invasion, Hitler turned his forces to a sustained bombing campaign. On 11th May 1941 London saw its worst night of bombing. Miss E M Wing of Eaton Ave recalls the night and the red glow of the sky in the capital burned. Harold Garner of Wavendon watched a similar glow in the north and remembers his mother wondering who was on the receiving end. The radio the next morning announced for night of devastation suffered by Coventry.

In Bletchley a rota was indeed organised for the ladies of the home front to spend their nights fire watching. Fortunately their skills were never put to the test, it is difficult to see how these two stationed at the south end of Bletchley Road (Queensway) would have coped with their one pump and twelve assorted galvanised buckets ! But throughout all, spirits remained very high. At the end of March 1942 Bletchley held a Warship Week to raise finance in support for the Royal Navy. A concert in the school raised £33 pounds which was donated to the cause.

The SS Chellwood's crew responded the next March presenting a cup to be used for house competitions. They also gave the school the casing from a shell that fired to bring down an enemy aircraft.

But no further mention is made in the school log of the Chellwood after 22nd May 1942 when it seems likely that she was lost to enemy action. From then on until the end of the war the school directed his attentions and efforts towards the RAF.

Ernest Cook threw his school wholeheartedly behind the war effort of which the Chellwood was just a part. Visits were made from General de Gaulle's office to teach the children about the activities of the Free French. Before the outbreak of the war there had been school visits to Paris and the children kept up a keen interest in the events of occupation. On 12th March 1946 a number of the former French underground spent time visiting the school, sharing experiences of the occupation and French resistance.

Thirty year update – We ARE The Concrete Cows:
As we talk about Bletchley today we must remember in the First World War years of 1914 and 1918 West Bletchley was farmland, most of the houses were in Fenny Stratford and Central Bletchley was very different.

As I write I have taken time away from my laptop to visit the war memorial in Fenny Stratford. Walking towards the memorial there is a low wall protruding from which are many small pieces of iron. They have been roughly cut, cut when the iron fence was removed, taken away and melted down to aid war weapons production. This remains eighty years later as a reminder of the war years here in Milton Keynes.

Bletchley and Fenny Stratford Council has some very special information regarding the war memorial. It was my original intention to precis this but to do so I feel would be to do an injustice so the following is exactly as it appear on the council's website.

The aftermath of the First World War saw the biggest single wave of public commemoration ever with tens of thousands of memorials erected across England. This was the result of both the huge impact on communities of the loss of three quarters of a million British lives, and also the official policy of not repatriating the dead which meant that the memorials provided the main focus of the grief felt at this great loss. One such memorial was raised at Fenny Stratford as a permanent testament to the sacrifice made by 69 members of the local community who lost their lives in the First World War.

Bletchley Urban District Council agreed that each of the three Parishes within its administrative area (Central Bletchley, Old Bletchley, and Water Eaton and Simpson) should construct its own memorial. The Chairman of Bletchley Urban District Council called a meeting on 13th February 1919 to discuss both a suitable memorial and the peace celebrations. A number of suggestions were made for the former including a stone memorial, an institute and a library: a sub-committee was formed to take the matter forward.

The sub-committee duly considered the matter on 6th March and it was agreed to consult the Urban District Council's surveyor, Major John Chadwick. A site was suggested on the Bletchley Road between the Council offices (at the junction of Queensway and Victoria

Road) and Messrs Randall's foundry (in Cambridge Street).
At a meeting held on 11th March there was a long discussion about a scheme for a hall with public baths, which Chadwick estimated at £5,500. This figure was twice the pre-war cost and Chadwick's figures were questioned, with some of the members thinking that the sum might fall to £3,500. The meeting was adjourned as those present felt unable to make a decision.

The matter lay in abeyance until a meeting of the War and Peace Celebrations Joint Committee on 29th August, when someone present called for a cenotaph on the lines of the one erected in London. A vote was taken.

Sir Herbert Leon, a noted local politician and public benefactor, called a Town Meeting on 5th September to consider or reject a proposal for a memorial consisting of either a cenotaph or an obelisk. Major Chadwick was subsequently asked to prepare a design and he gave his services voluntarily.

A meeting of the Committee on 3rd February 1920 considered Chadwick's design and, while granite was preferred, at £200 Portland stone would be some £140 cheaper. It was agreed to transfer £123 from the Peace Celebrations funds. The War Memorial Committee for Old Bletchley asked for the return of £19 that it had provided for the Peace Celebrations, raised from door-to-door collections. The committee decided to refuse this application, because no detailed records had been kept concerning the precise source of the money. There was a slight change to the proposed location for the memorial, which was to be in front of the boys' department of the Bletchley Road Council Schools (also designed by Major Chadwick).

Construction work duly started and, in November 1920, it was reported that the substructure should be complete by the end of the year. The builder was Messrs Yirrell of Leighton Buzzard and the memorial was dedicated on 8th January 1921 by Colonel P Broome Giles.

A paved path and stone wall were built at a cost of £10 6s 6d in 1922, funded from the balance in the Memorial Funds account. The work was supplemented by a footpath, chains, and gates in July 1927 costing £8 10s, using surplus money in the account together with £5 15s donated by the Women's Section of the British Legion, which had decided to close. At a ceremony to mark the completion of the gates, the ribbon was cut by Lady Leon.

Following the Second World War, the names of twenty-five local servicemen who died in that conflict were added to the memorial.

MUMS ARMY:

Although rationing was a difficulty to be endured by everyone each and every person was making a specific contribution to the war effort.

At the outbreak of war Britain imported something in excess of 40% and then a year later it was down to 30%. Even so strict rationing was essential. Butter, sugar, bacon and ham were the first commodities to be controlled with meat being added in March 1940, jam and tined fruit in March 1941, cheese in April of that year and eggs in May. By the summer of 1943 the personal weekly ration food included four ounces of meat, one ounce of cheese, eight ounces of lard, four ounces of sugar, four ounces of jam and one ounce of powdered egg.

The MODERN ILLUSTRATED COOK BOOK of 1940 proffered some good advice as well as an encyclopaedia of recipes. *Economy is the keynote of modern cookery - the true economy which means not going short of food, but using every scrap to the very best advantage. Nowadays it is more a question of making the most of what is available than choosing what we prefer. Make friends with your shopkeepers and help them in every way you can - remember they, as well as you, are having a difficult time.*

As well as digging up the flower gardens to grow food, homes in Milton Keynes took on allotments in order to expand the domestic production and supplement rationing. As well as growing vegetables, pigs and poultry became common on the domestic scene with animals being reared in the back garden.

Schools set pupils to work digging up every spare part of their ground in order to plant vegetables. A rural study centre was opened on the site now occupied by the Bletchley campus of Milton Keynes college. In fact it resembled a small farm with different schools sending children to work there.

Bletchley Road School's headmaster recorded details of the work and harvests in the school logbook. He was able to discuss his schools work with Lord Wootton, the

Minister of Food, in the autumn of 1942 when he could report some very fine results.

Fenny Stratford Magistrates ordered, in late 1939, that two boys who had stolen a laying hen from the Bletchley allotment, to be birched six times ! Meanwhile Aylesbury Crown Court sentenced a worker at Tetley's Watling Street factory to three months imprisonment for stealing tea and selling it to friends. Harsh punishments !

Among the wartime immigrants to Milton Keynes were members of the Women's Land Army. Originally formed during the First World War, it was reformed in June 1939 when nearly 100,000 enrolled nationwide for this work with a significant number of young girls from the industrial cities coming to rural North Buckinghamshire in order to replace the farm workers who left to join the forces. Dormitory accommodation was provided in huts just off Church Green Road, Bletchley, from where the ladies were bussed out each day to surrounding farms. My late mother-in-law came to Wavendon to work as a land army girl.

It may have been an accident of planning or an intentional morale boost to situate the Land Army base adjacent to an RAF signals camp. It is reported that many friendly encounters were enjoyed between the two establishments !

Home Farm, in Newton Longville, kept by George Tofield, did not use land army girls but Italian prisoners of war. His daughter Daphne, a young girl at the time, remembers these men being brought in to work at harvest and remains in contact with one of them, Dante Servi who worked on her uncles land at Thatchams Pond Farm and, now in his seventies, still lives in the area. She also recalls the regular visits paid to the farm by ministry inspectors. If they found the land being inefficiently maintained the farmer faced eviction to make way for someone who could better serve the war effort. Under the management of Farmer Tofield Home Farm was always classed as A ONE PLUS.

For those who, like me, were not born until well after the end of World War Two it is not easy to comprehend the spirit that pervaded between 1939 and 1945. How amidst the austerity and fear of the future ordinary people were not only able to cope but to unite in a common cause in a miracle itself. From the child digging in the school garden to his father fighting in North Africa, from the city girl tilling the land to the housewife making the best meal possible from the meanest of ingredients, all had a part to play and all did it way beyond the best of their abilities.

TRY THESE WARTIME RECIPES:

Cabbage and onion soup: 1 spring cabbage 1 medium onion 1 meat cube ½ pint of milk salt and pepper 1 dessertspoon of flour 2 pints of water. Wash and trim the cabbage and onions, then let them soak for half an hour in cold water. Take them out and drain. Bring the water to the boil, add a teaspoon of salt, put in the cabbage and onions. Simmer in an open pan until the cabbage is tender. Strain the vegetables, reserving the water in which they were boiled. Remove the heart of the cabbage to use for another dish. Chop the reminder of the onions very finely. Dissolve the meat cube in the vegetable water. Mix the flour with a little milk then stir it in and continue stirring until it has boiled for five minutes. Add the chopped onion to the milk. Bring to the boil and serve at once.

Toad in the hole without eggs: ½ pint of milk 4 ounces of plain flour ½ a teaspoon of bicarbonate of soda 1 teaspoon of vinegar a good pinch of salt ½ a pound of small sausages ½ an ounce of dripping or margarines cooking time about 30 minutes on gas mark four or electricity 375. Mix the salt with the flower. Grease the baking dish. Stir bicarbonate of soda into the milk and dissolve it. Then add it gradually to the flower, stirring gently all the time. Add the vinegar. Put the sausages in the greased tin, pour the batter over and bake it once in a moderate oven. Remember to put it into the oven as soon as the batter is made. The lightness of this dish depends upon the batter and the bicarbonate of soda loses its power when the moisture is added.

Cauliflower scallops: 1 cauliflower ¼ pounder potatoes 2 ounces of butter one gill (1/8 of a pint of milk) pepper and salt cooking time 30 minutes on gas mark six electricity 425. Take the leaves away from the cauliflower and boil the flower in salted water until it is quite tender. Break it into small pieces. Boil the potatoes and mash them, beat them well with butter, milk, pepper and salt. Mix this with the cauliflower. Fill small fireproof moulds with the mixture. Pile a little mash potato on the top to ornament. Bake until brown in a hot oven.

When these recipes first appeared on my page in the Milton Keynes Citizen I was inundated with requests for more examples of those recorded in the cookery books of the time. One lady planned a 1940's meal for her mother as a birthday celebration. Mrs Barnard Cranfield tried out the toad in the hole saying it was quite tasty although she doubted how easy the sausages would have been available during the years of rationing.

A SERIES OF NEAR MISSES:

In 1939, at the outbreak of World War II, Harold Holdness of Shenley Road Bletchley was a train driver on the LMS Railway. He was in a reserved occupation and so served his country from the footplate of a railway engine. But his was just as dangerous a war as those in any of the forces.

Railways were an obvious target for the Luftwaffe and, while the area now covered by Milton Keynes was spared the bombing, Harold knew that when he took his train north of Wolverton or south of Leighton Buzzard he was moving into dangerous areas. On one occasion, just outside Northampton, an enemy aircraft straddled the line with three bombs. On another a shadow fell across his cab, Harold and his fireman threw themselves to the floor of their engine as a Messerschmitt buzzed the Bletchley to Oxford train. The aircraft was so low that Harold could see his pilot laughing as he passed overhead.

Winston Churchill was a regular visitor to Bletchley, as were General Montgomery and in the later years of war General Eisenhower, Supreme Allied Commander Europe. They made secret visits to Bletchley Park decoding centre of British Intelligence. Harold was never told when he had a VIP on board or the identity of his special passenger, being only aware by the extra, and highly guarded carriage coupled to his train.

Looking back Harold wonders which made him more nervous, the German Air Force or having the life of the Prime Minister entrusted to his charge !

Mrs Bramma of Newport Pagnell was born and brought up in the village of Chicheley and was nine years old when war broke out. She recalls how a couple of fields away a large Anderson shelter was built and huge lights placed around the field. The children were forbidden to go anywhere near but crept around the hedgerows to have a peep. Sometimes at night lights flashed and on a few occasions bombs were dropped on the field. The dummy airfield was intended to draw aircraft away from Cranfield.

AN UNWELCOME SUNDAY GUEST:

Villagers to the south of Milton Keynes became used to their Sunday afternoons being disturbed on something of a regular basis by an enemy reconnaissance plane. The aircraft, a white Dornier, would fly so low that its markings were clearly visible from the ground and became known locally as Jerry Sunday. Apparently, it was taking pictures of the aerodrome construction near to Wing.

One Sunday, Fighter Command was waiting for it in the shape of two Hurricanes. The Dornier was shot down near Great Brickhill and the peace of Sunday afternoons was returned

Another lone enemy aircraft dropped a single bomb on Stoke Road, Newton Longville early one autumn morning. It seems rather strange that this particular attack could have taken place for the nearest strategic target was miles away ! Daphne Capp, whose parents kept Home Farm in the village, remembers the bomb and how the ground shook like an earthquake. The crater remained in the field for many years.

ALMOST AN OWN GOAL:

The railway had its own platoon of Home Guard whose headquarters lay between the line and the present-day Saxon Street. One evening a group of men were being drilled in the use of the new consignment of rifles when one was accidentally fired. The bullet passed right through the wooden wall narrowly missing two men standing outside sharing the cigarette !

Oops !

ENEMY AIRCRAFT IN SCHOOL PLAYGROUND:

A model Messerschmitt in the playground at Bletchley Road School attracted many visitors whose entrance fees totalled £44-1-3d which was donated to the Bletchley War Weapons week. During May 1941 the townsfolk raised a staggering £88,859 ! (After inflation, by today's standards this would be well in excess of £1,000,000 - I wrote that originally in 1994 goodness knows what it be worth today)

Just about every business, church, club and school was mobilised towards the war effort. All this from the population which was a tiny fraction of modern-day

Milton Keynes. Children in the school raised alone raised £443-18-0d !

Regulars of a nearby pub at Maulden took up a collection in the bar raising £75 which they forwarded to Bomber Command requesting it be used to pay for a bomb to be dropped on Berlin.

THE NEAREST MISS OF ALL:

Bletchley Park dates back to the Doomsday Book, passing through a variety of owners until, on the death of Fanny Lady Leon in 1937, it was split up and sold in lots. The area of land between Saint Mary's Church and the railway was taken over by the government, during the war years to become the most closely guarded secret. Hundreds of cryptologists beavered away breaking the codes of intercepted enemy messages totally unknown to German Intelligence. The fact that this massive operation was kept a secret is one of the greatest achievements of the war. Had Hitler ever found out what was going on he would have ordered the total destruction of Bletchley.

Nancy Holdness came from London to work in Bletchley Park and recalls the armed guards on the gate and how, even years after the war ended, she was still bound by the Official Secrets Act. An attitude existed amongst the general population that totally discouraged the asking of any questions related to anything to do with the military and so the people of Bletchley went about their daily business not stopping to think of the work going on at Bletchley Park. This cannot have been an entirely easy thing to do for many of the characters employed there were decidedly eccentric and stood out amongst other residents in the area. There was one university professor in particular who used to walkabout the shops wearing his shirt always outside his trousers. Not significant today but quite strange in 1942.

A local journalist of the time recalls how everybody was aware that there was top secret work going on but never thought to ask what it was. Fred Morton knows his father received an OBE for his work at Bletchley Park but has no idea at all what he did. Thank goodness the Gestapo never sent any spies to North Buckinghamshire. This oversight has to be one of the closest shaves of all time.

THE HERITAGE OF A NAME

Have you ever stopped to wonder why your street or estate takes the name afforded to it ? Just why is there a Grafton Street and what was the reason why Coffee Hall is so named ?

In the days before the Milton Keynes Development Corporation the assortment of local authorities adopted a haphazard method naming roads after rivers, trees, castles or whatever first came to mind. However, the central planners of the New City employed a more deliberate system, diligently applying names significant to the development. A careful record, I understand, was maintained but attempts to secure a copy from both the borough council and the Commission for New Town's drew a blank ! But my curiosity was aroused and so I thought I set off on a detective trail to re discover the stories behind some of our roads and the local areas about them.

Glancing at the map of the city Saxon Street, the V7, stretching from its junction with Buckingham Road in Bletchley, all the way to Newport Road is Stantonbury in the North, seemed an ideal point about which to begin.

Bletchley has its origins, at least as far as its name is concerned, in the Anglo-Saxon era as Beccas Lea - Lea meaning open ground, meadow or clearing. Becca was probably the name of the earliest Saxon settlers in the area.

Bletcham Way. To the right is Mount Farm Lake which originates from an old gravel pit on the Mount Farm which used to lay between Watling Street and the Grand Junction Canal.

Land to the south of the old Roman Road and adjacent on either side to Saxon Street upon which now stands in the assortment of factories and the Tesco superstore was once part of Denbigh Hall Farm and put up for sale and development in 1936 by Fanny Lady Leon of Bletchley Park. (Research since I wrote this text enabled me to explain Lady Leon did not sell the ground for profit but to bring industry and employment to the area.)

Crossing Groveway, (the H9 grid road) set down in 1781 to link Denbigh Hall on the Watling Street with Simpson Road, Saxon Street passes the sites of three fields named in 1781: Beanhill Close Field, Ashlands Field and Nether Field, nether meaning lower. All this took place during the enclosure from the open field system, a process that began in Milton Keynes in the late 1500's and continued to 1845.

To the left was the site of Coffee Hall Farm and beyond that Old Brook Field designated in 1850.

Not all were in favour of the enclosures brought about by the Agrarian Revolution. Reverend William Cole, Rector of Bletchley from 1753 to 1767, was overwhelmingly opposed to the change while Arthur Young, the celebrated agriculturist and exponent of the new methods, declared how ideal the surrounding land and makeup of the soil was to the more intensified method of farming.

But the enclosure movement would not go away and it changed the face of the countryside beyond all recognition. Where there had once been wide open plains there now came a patchwork quilt of smaller fields all of which needed to be named. Several of those names from the agricultural revolution live on being passed to the development of Milton Keynes.

Crossing the H6 Child's Way and H5 Portway, Saxon Street passes two roads much, much older than the New City. Childs Way was put down in 1769 taking its name from the adjacent Childs Field which was directly North of Old Brook Field. Portway, however, is considerably older dating back to 1250.

Saxon government was organised by regions known as hundreds. The Sigelai or Seckloe Hundred basically encompassed all of the city to the west of the River Ouzel while the Brickhills, Milton Keynes Village, Broughton, Moulsoe and Tickford were within the Moulsoe Hundreds.

The part of the city we now call Central Milton Keynes

was of no mean significance in the Saxon age and has given us the name of Saxon Street. Behind the library is Secklow Mound dating from AD 914. This was the site of the ancient Saxon moot or seat of government and it was no coincidence that planners designated it for the focus (In the original text I used the word hub but sadly in Central Milton Keynes that word has taken on a different meaning) of the New City. Just as it did over one thousand years ago, the high elevation enables a centre to be viewed from the surrounding lands.

The moot was probably held every month and was a centre of great activity. As well as those bringing cases to trial and political discussions there would have been itinerant merchants peddling ale, bread, cheese and a dozen other wares.

From AD 457 to AD 827 Britain was divided into seven Anglo Saxon kingdoms. Milton Keynes came under the Kingdom of Mercia which stretched from the Mersey to the Thames.

During the building of the city Saxon remains were excavated all over the area, evidence of a hall was found at Pennylands, jewellery at Great Linford, coinage at Shenley Church End and the grave of a woman in Newport Pagnell.

Continuing our journey beyond the city centre, Conniburrow takes its name from Connie Borough Hill named in 1641. A connie, of course, is a rabbit but the original spelling of the field used Burrough, derived from the Saxon meaning a sheltered place and not a borrow meaning warren. Away to the north-west were two more fields, again from 1641, Briar Hedge Field and Long Neath Hill. While the former appears forgotten the latter of course lives on.

Linford Wood dates from 1283 and was originally at deer park. About half a mile to the north-west of the wood was Calare's Farm also known as Stanton High Farm. Not to be confused with Stantonbury Farm which was north of the Stony Stratford to Newport Pagnell Turnpike. The bury in Stantonbury is again a Saxon word meaning a fortified place, offering further evidence of the Saxon influence, although there is evidence of a Roman Villa on the site from several hundred years earlier.

Stantonbury brings us to the end of our northward drive. Now we will start across the city from West to East along Standing Way.

The actual naming of Standing Way is somewhat obscure and I have been unable to trace its origin. I do, however, have a theory although perhaps unlikely, so unless a reader can put forward something more accurate I will stick with this explanation.

The 4th Baronet of Bletchley Park and great grandson of Sir Herbert Leon, is Sir John Leon. I have known John since before I started writing Not The Concrete Cows. Sir John has never lived in Milton Keynes having made homes in London, Los Angeles and Surrey, it is possible he is the name behind Standing Way, Sir John is better known as John Standing the film and television actor.

Standing was his mother's maiden name before she married Sir Ronald Leon. As an actress herself she was Kate Hammond and it was for her that Noel Coward fashioned the character of Elvira in Blithe Spirit. As well as acting the part on stage Kate played Elvira opposite Rex Harrison in the film version.

I put my theory to Sir John, who is married to the daughter of Sir Brian Forbes and Nanette Newman with three lovely children, but he was every bit as sceptical as I am.

Anyway, to get back to our journey along Standing Way. The A421 connects Buckingham with Bedford, until the emergence of Aylesbury the original two county towns, by way of Milton Keynes. It enters the city at the Bottle Dump where it becomes Standing Way.

To the south is Newton Longville. Newton comes from the Saxon but long Longville refers to the Norman Lord the Manor. The Lord of Longville in Northern France had provided thirty ships for the invasion and was commander of the Norman army at the Battle of Hastings. His son, Walter, was Commissioner of The Doomsday Survey and founder of the Newton Longville Priory.

The Bottle Dump at the junction of the road to Newton Longville became something of a legend in its own time as an early recycling centre. Many a resident can remember taking glass bottles along the Buckingham Road to the dump. It's trademark was the bottles hanging from strings in its trees. To the newcomer the roundabout on Standing Way named Bottle Dump is something of an enigma but to those who lived in Bletchley prior to the coming of Milton Keynes Development Corporation it is an eccentric but valued part of our heritage.

The first of the city grid roads to connect Standing Way is Snelshall Street, V1.

Snelshall Priory was founded in 1150 and was situated slightly to the south of Oakhill Wood, as a home for Premonstratensian Cannons becoming a home to Benedictine Monks. When it was surrendered to the dissolution in 1535 it was wholly in ruins.

Many of the stones from Snelshall Priory were employed five years later in the building of Tattenhoe Church adjacent to Howe Park Wood The hoe in Tattenhoe is another Saxon word which means spur of land. The village steadily declined after the consecration of the church until the coming of the New City it had almost disappeared. However, the development of Milton Keynes has secured its future again as a thriving community.

Howe Park Wood possibly originates from woodland set down at the end of the last Ice Age. It is believed one particular oak tree is the oldest living thing in the city.

To the south of Standing Way is Windmill Hill Golf Course, opened in the early 1970's by Bletchley Urban District Council. The naming of the course and surrounding housing development comes from Tattenhoe Windmill which stood on the site from the mid thirteenth century. At three hundred and seventy-two feet above sea level this is the highest point in the parish and was a perfect location for a windmill which remained in existence for several centuries but was probably spelt Wymmyllehull rather than that 20th century Windmill Hill.

During the period of the enclosures among the new farms defined was Valley Farm in about 1600 and Emerson's Farm 100 years later. Hence Emerson Valley.

Moving towards the Watling Street is the housing estate of Furzton This name was taken from the Iron Age settlement known to have existed there some three hundred years before the birth of Christ. A spearhead from the much later Saxon period was discovered there during building work in 1975.

Standing Way crosses Watling Street at Denbigh Hall, the site of the local gallows in the mid seventeenth century. It was also the location of the infamous Denby Hall Inn notorious for harbouring highway men and just about every other kind of criminal imaginable.

Between April 1838 and September of that year it was the southern terminus of the railway. Until the completion of the Wolverton Viaduct and Kilsby Tunnel passengers were carried forward by stagecoach.

To the north where Elfield Common Field and Loughton Clay Pit. The latter is now the National Bowl and has hosted concerts by Queen, David Bowie, Michael Jackson and the Royal Philharmonic Orchestra. As they entertained vast crowds I wonder what Freddie Mercury, Brian May, Roger Taylor, John Deacon, David Bowie and Michael Jackson thought of this Milton Keynes place where they had come to perform.

Continuing eastwards on Standing Way we pass Coffee Hall Farm and its fields of Beanhill Close, Ashlands and Netherfield all named in 1781.

From the rise alongside Milton Keynes General Hospital it is possible to see across Woughton, Walton, Kents Hill and as far as Brogborough Hill in adjacent Bedfordshire. Today it is hard to picture the area as open farmland, without the City of Milton Keynes. It is even harder to imagine everything as wide-open land, minus hedges, fence nothing but uninterrupted ripening corn before the acts of enclosure.

The UK population at the time was around ten and a half million. Today it is just under sixty-eight million. The population of Milton Keynes is almost quarter of a million. It is so difficult to compare these times. What would those who lived where we now live make of Milton Keynes ? I think we would get almost as many different opinions as there were people.

There was evidence of Iron Age Settlements in Woughton and the area has been steeped in history and legend ever since. Turpyn Court takes the name not from the highwayman Dick Turpin who used to lodge at the Swan Inn but from the Reverend Henry Turpyn the local witch finder general and seeker out of evil. A gibbet used to be sited opposite the church and may be the source of at least some of the ghosts reputed to haunt the village.

South Standing Way is the point on our on our journey of Walton Hall, home to the world-famous Open University. The house was originally built as a private home and was taken over by the University in 1972.

It was perhaps the Open University that first put Milton Keynes on the map but it totally decimated the village of Walton and the deconsecrating of Saint Michael Church which is now a lecture Hall. Perhaps The Open

University could set up a project to consider present-day Milton Keynes and place it alongside the thinking of the different people who resided here in times before our own.

Adjoining the Open University is de Montfort University taking its name from Simon de Monfort. Simon de Montfort was the Earl of Leicester and lived between 1208 and 1268. He was considered a hero even in his own day and he is regarded by history as a significant father of parliament. The tyrannous incompetence of Henry VIII made the barons determined not to lose the benefits secured in Magna Carta. The outstanding character of Simon made him their natural leader. The Milton Keynes campus, allied to Leicester University, proudly takes his name.

Making a trilogy of learning is the BT Regional Training Centre relocated from Bletchley Park. Standing Way here passes through the former grounds of Kent House dating from 1680, and giving us the name of Kents Hill. The adjoining industrial area of Brinklow is named after Brinklow Hill Field enclosed in1685.

Tesco Supermarket, McDonald's and a wealth of retailing establishments making up Kingston Centre are sited upon the land which was once part of Pinchcote Farm, The name of Kingston comes from the Kings Highway which was the Hockcliffe to Newport Pagnell Turnpike.

Beyond Kingston is Milton Keynes Village which the planners would now like us to call Middleton. But why should this village suffer loss of its identity after giving its name to the New City ?

Milton probably has its origins in the Saxon TUN or TONE meaning and enclosed farm and may indeed have been called Middleton. Keynes was grafted on later as that of the name of an early Lord of the Manor.

Milton Keynes Village was part of Queen Edith's estate, the wife of Edward the Confessor. When her husband lay dying he commended her to the care of Harold but in 1066 she firmly supported William. On her death in 1075 the land passed to Godric. Edith was the daughter of Earl Godwin of Essex after whom we find Godwin Close in Wavendon Gate.

Beyond here the A421 becomes the Woburn Sands/Aspley Guise bypass swinging its congested way around to the M1 at Junction Thirteen, but I am going to head straight on and into Woburn Sands.

To the right of the road is Wavendon which in Saxon times was Wafa's Hill. The parishes of Wavendon and Woburn were larger than their present extent until 1865 when the parish of Woburn Sands was created. In his heyday Wavendon had several ends one of which was Hogsty End and it was this that became Woburn Sands. One of the reasons for the increasing importance of Woburn Sands can be found in the plague of 1665. Reverend Cole, Rector of Bletchley recorded in his diary..... *there died in the Bletchley part of Fenny Stratford about 106 persons and in the Simpson part of Fenny 23 which means that one in six or seven of the entire population died within the three months the plague or raged.*

Following the disease, travellers started to avoid Fenny Stratford leaving Watling Street at Hockliffe and journeying via Woburn, Hogsty End and Wavendon.

Although Woburn Sands was not created as a parish until the mid-nineteenth century the Quakers formed a meeting house there 200 years previously. This is now Woburn Sands Library. In 1682 seven persons were brought before the Aylesbury Quarter Sessions for failing to attend church over a period of three months. They were fined 42 pounds and 13 shillings.

It is arguable, of course, that Woburn Sands is not within Milton Keynes at all and in the early days of the New City many residents tried very hard to ignore the development going on down the road. However, it is now firmly within the borough as far as the county boundary with Bedfordshire.

AND FINALLY:
So that's it then, the end of our journey together through Milton Keynes. Anymore and will tumble out of the end of the book ! But please don't get me wrong there is a whole lot more that I could have written, and if the readers of the Milton Keynes Citizen don't tire of me I have enough material to keep me going for centuries, but may I suggest you go out into the highways and byways of the city and research it for yourself.

Go and look at some of the things I have noted in this little book. Go and find for yourself the windmill that never turns, stand in Queensway opposite Knowles School and let your mind imagine the lone bomber of Skew Bridge. Walk along Stony Stratford High Street and look for Queen Eleanor's funeral. Pack yourself a picnic and organise a day out in your hometown, there's lots and lots to see.

This is a good place to live, true enough parts of it are bad and some of it is even ugly but to us all it is home and for certain there is a whole lot more to Milton Keynes than just the concrete cows !

Enjoy it.

AND FINALLY AFTER THIRTY YEARS – We ARE The Concrete Cows:

What was it I said within the opening of this book, about my taking out a subscription to the Milton Keynes Fan Club ? Well here I am thirty years after writing Not The Concrete Cows and I hope my membership of our city's fan club is clear to all.

In January 1967 Harold Wilson's government dedicated an area of land in North Buckinghamshire for the building of a New City. In 1994 Not The Concrete Cows took readers through a kaleidoscope across our adolescent New City. Perhaps the word city should have been spelt with a small *c* as we did not have a city charter. Indeed from adolescence into adult life, celebrating its half century in 2017, Milton Keynes was not a city, it had not been awarded a city charter.

When a member of Milton Keynes Council was sounding off about our being granted a city charter I wrote to him offering to meet and share the writing you have just kaleidoscope through, that and more I had penned over the years. He did not reply ! SURPRISE, SURPRISE this is very much the norm for councillors here in Milton Keynes.

Frustrated, I sat down and penned a lengthy presentation of my own asking for Milton Keynes to be granted a city charter which I sent to Buckingham Palace. I do know that my extended letter was put before Her Majesty Queen Elizabeth II.

Unlike Milton Keynes City Councillors, staff at Buckingham Palace are able to read and write. I received a beautiful reply.

When within Her Late Majesty's Platinum Jubilee Milton Keynes was granted a city charter I had to pinch myself to check I was not dreaming. I wrote to Her Majesty saying THANK YOU. I received a reply saying THANK YOU FOR SAYING THANK YOU !

Did my presentation to Buckingham Palace help our concrete cows to become residents of a real city ? I do not know and in all honesty it does not matter. What I do know is how proud I am to have made Milton Keynes my adopted home, a home which is a lot more than Concrete Cows.

David Ashford Formerly writing under the pen-name of Jonathan Flie

Printed in Great Britain
by Amazon

50357596R00106